6

5

4

The first to perish were the children . . .
From these . . . our new dawn might have risen.

Yitzhak Katzenelson
poet, playwright, and educator (1886 – 1944)

Tell Them We Remember

3

1

2

Tell Them We Remember

The Story of the Holocaust

Susan D. Bachrach

UNITED STATES HOLOCAUST MEMORIAL MUSEUM

LITTLE, BROWN AND COMPANY

New York Boston

Little, Brown and Company

Hachette Book Group
237 Park Avenue, New York, NY 10017
Visit our website at www.lb-kids.com

Little, Brown and Company is a division of Hachette Book Group, Inc.
The Little, Brown name and logo are trademarks of Hachette Book Group, Inc.

First Edition: October 1994

Library of Congress Cataloging-in-Publication Data
Bachrach, Susan D.
Tell them we remember: the story of the Holocaust / by Susan D. Bachrach. —1st ed.
p.   cm.
Includes bibliographical references and index.
ISBN 978-0-316-69264-9 (hc)
ISBN 978-0-316-07484-1 (pb)
1. Holocaust, Jewish (1939–1945) — Juvenile literature. 2. World
War, 1939–1945 — Children — Juvenile literature. 3. Jewish children —
Juvenile literature. 4. Holocaust, Jewish (1939–1945) —
Exhibitions — Juvenile literature. 5. U.S. Holocaust Memorial
Museum — Exhibitions — Juvenile literature. [1. Holocaust, Jewish
(1939–1945) 2. World War, 1939–1945. 3. U.S. Holocaust Memorial
Museum.] I. U.S. Holocaust Memorial Museum. II. Title.
D804.53'18—dc20   93-40090

25 24 23 22 21

Printed in the United States of America

Title page photograph: Young survivors of Buchenwald concentration camp. Buchenwald, Germany, 1945. Fédération Nationale des Deportés et Internés Resistants, Paris, France.

Photographs on pages ii–iii and 110–111

These photographs show the importance and diversity of family life before the Holocaust. Most of them were taken in the 1930s, before the Nazis and their collaborators carried out the mass murder of Jews and Gypsies. Many of the photographs are formal portraits of Jewish families from various countries in Europe. Two photographs of Gypsy families are also included.

Many individuals shown here, from babies to grandparents, were killed during the Holocaust. In many instances, surviving family members donated the photographs to the United States Holocaust Memorial Museum.

1. The extended family of Nesanya and Sura Ratzer. Gewovdziec, Poland, 1934. *Donated by Shirley Willing Koperberg.* USHMM.

2. The Fischer family. Beregszasz, Hungary, 1932. *Donated by M. Deutsch.* USHMM.

3. Else Kahn Schyveschuurder with her two stepsons, Joseph, age 11, and Louis, age 6. Haarlem, Netherlands, 1933. *Donated by Yoseph Schyveschuurder.* USHMM.

4. Naftali and Rosa Krauthamer with their two children, Simon, age 2, and Jules, age 1. Hannover, Germany, c. 1934. *Donated by Simon Krauthamer.* USHMM.

5. The children of the chief of the Turkish Gypsies in Turnu-Măgurele, Romania, 1930s. *Institut Ag. in Leipzig, Leipzig, Germany.*

6. The family of Menahem Salem, with his seven daughters, their husbands, and children. Larissa, Greece, c. 1936. *Gift of Rebecca Mayo. Yaffa Eliach Collection, Museum of Jewish Heritage, New York, N.Y.*

7. The Rzondzinski family. Kałuszyn, Poland, c. 1930. *Donated by Michael Kishel.* USHMM.

8. The Gelb family. Khust, Czechoslovakia, c. 1937. *Gift of Olga Abraham. Yaffa Eliach Collection, Museum of Jewish Heritage, New York, N.Y.*

9. The Weinmann family. Vienna, Austria, c. 1939. *Donated by Hans R. Weinmann.* USHMM.

10. The Jacobowitz family. Rachov, Czechoslovakia, c. 1929. *Gift of Morris Gottesman. Yaffa Eliach Collection, Museum of Jewish Heritage, New York, N.Y.*

11. The Lische family. Debica, Poland, 1935. *Donated by Norman Salsitz.* USHMM.

12. The Stojka family, detained for registration in a Gypsy internment camp. Vienna, Austria, 1940. *Bundesarchiv, Koblenz, Germany.*

ACKNOWLEDGMENTS

In preparing this book, I have drawn on many resources developed and maintained by the staff of the United States Holocaust Memorial Museum. It is a pleasure to work with colleagues so dedicated to the educational mission of the museum.

A number of staff members deserve special mention for their contributions to this book.

William Parsons, director of education for children and schools, gave me the job of writing this book and provided advice, encouragement, and support throughout the project. Cheering me on in many ways were my other colleagues on the education staff: Kristy Brosius, Karen Jacobs, David Klevan, Marcia Sabol, Marilyn Thomas, Dawn Marie Warfle, and Shari Rosenstein Werb.

Arnold Kramer, director of technical services at the museum, took all the photographs of artifacts included in the book. His assistant, Beth Redlich, has been very helpful. Genya Markon, director of photo archives, Teresa Amiel Pollin, Andrew Campana, and Vivian Boxer provided the historical photos. Dewey Hicks and William Meinecke provided the maps. Bill Connelly and Steve Vitto of the museum's library staff, directed by Elizabeth Koenig, offered their usual cheerful assistance. Karen Wyatt assisted with copyrights. Jeffrey LaRiche helped resolve other legal issues.

Several members of the museum staff read the manuscript with great care, and I appreciate their attention: Jeshajahu Weinberg, director of the museum; Sara Bloomfield, director of public programs; Michael Berenbaum, director of the research institute; Sybil Milton, senior historian in the research institute; Stephen Goodell, director of education for special audiences; and Severin Hochberg, director of education for adult and community programs. Peggy Obrecht, director for church relations, also read part of the manuscript.

The many comments and questions of these readers have deepened my knowledge and understanding of Holocaust history. I have incorporated their suggested revisions wherever it was possible to do so and still have a text comprehensible to younger readers. Writing for this audience presented a special challenge.

Stephanie Owens Lurie, senior editor in Little, Brown's children and young adult division, did an excellent job shaping the text to make it more accessible to younger readers. Working with her has been a pleasure, and I am grateful for having had such an experienced editor. I owe thanks, too, to managing editor Jackie Horne, copyeditor Betty Power, and designer Anne Moore.

I would also like to acknowledge my former colleagues from the identity card project, which produced the I.D. stories used throughout this book. Pamela Kidron, director of the project, was an intelligent editor who taught me a great deal about writing about the Holocaust for a general audience. Carmit Kurn provided invaluable assistance to the project as did Norma Tash and many volunteer transcribers. Fellow writers Tony Di Iorio, Sharon Tash, Tony Young, and Kevin Wayne each brought special talents to the project. Klaus Mueller of the University of Amsterdam also worked closely with us.

Our work in the I.D. project depended on the cooperation of many Holocaust survivors who gave us extensive oral histories now on deposit in the oral history archives. Their very abbreviated stories provided on the I.D. cards have helped visitors to the museum transcend the impersonal and staggering statistics of Holocaust victims. All the survivors I worked with, as well as some of their relatives, gave me invaluable personal perspectives on the Holocaust. My special thanks go to Michael Kishel, who has talked freely to me on many occasions about what it was like to be a Jewish teenager living in the Warsaw region in the 1930s and about the details of his ordeal, including the loss of many of his relatives, during the Holocaust.

Immersion in the history of the Holocaust has made me appreciate more than ever the importance of friends and family. I am grateful for the love and security my parents have always provided, and for the comforts, challenges, and joys of living with Peter, Annie, and Ben.

Susan D. Bachrach
United States Holocaust Memorial Museum
Washington, D.C.
September 30, 1993

Contents

**Part Three
Rescue, Resistance,
and Liberation**

Introduction

The United States Holocaust Memorial Museum is America's national institution for the study of Holocaust history and serves as this country's memorial to the millions of people murdered during the Holocaust.

What does *holocaust* mean? The word comes from the Greek, and originally meant a sacrifice totally burned by fire. Today people sometimes use the word *holocaust* to describe the slaughter of human beings on a large scale. Specifically, *Holocaust* refers to the murder of six million Jews, as well as the persecution and murder of millions of other innocent people by Nazi Germany and its supporters between 1933 and 1945.

Although this book cannot cover everything that happened during the Holocaust, because millions of people in dozens of nations were involved, we hope that what you find in these pages will give you a sense of how the lives of people throughout Europe were affected. The book reproduces materials from the museum's large collection of artifacts, photographs, maps, and taped oral and video histories provided by Holocaust survivors and other witnesses. It also includes excerpts from "identity cards" that are part of the museum's exhibit. Each identity card presented in the book focuses on the specific story of a young person who suffered or died during the Holocaust.

Before the Holocaust, these young people enjoyed a world that revolved around their families and friends, and school and play. When they became trapped under Nazi rule, their worlds were turned upside down. Children and teenagers were uprooted from their homes and often torn from their parents. Their hopes for the future evaporated, and they lived in fear.

More than one million children and teenagers were murdered by the Germans. The overwhelming majority of them were Jewish. Thousands of Roma (Gypsy) children, disabled children, and Polish Catholic children were also among the victims. Like their parents, they were singled out not for anything they had done, but simply because the Nazis considered them inferior.

The young people who survived to become adults passed on the stories of relatives and friends who had been killed, with the hope that the terrible crimes of the Holocaust would never be forgotten or repeated. The United States Holocaust Memorial Museum was created with the same hope. May the photographs and stories offered here remind us of the many young people who were never given a chance to grow up.

Jeshajahu Weinberg, Director (1989–1995)
United States Holocaust Memorial Museum

United States Holocaust
Memorial Museum. The museum
was officially dedicated by
President Bill Clinton on April 22,
1993. *Photo:* USHMM.

I.D. Photo Guide

Note: Stories of these individuals appear throughout this book. Many of these I.D. photos will appear more than once, as the reader follows each individual story as it unfolds at different points in time from 1933 to 1945.

Name: Barbara Ledermann
Date of birth: September 4, 1925
Place of birth: Berlin, Germany

Name: Wolfgang Munzer
Date of birth: February 26, 1920
Place of birth: Berlin, Germany

Name: Susanne Ledermann
Date of birth: October 8, 1928
Place of birth: Berlin, Germany

Name: Joseph Muscha Müller
Date of birth: 1931
Place of birth: Bitterfeld, Germany

Name: Idzia Pienknawiesz
Date of birth: 1920
Place of birth: Kałuszyn, Poland

Name: Gad Beck
Date of birth: 1923
Place of birth: Berlin, Germany

Name: Joseph Gani
Date of birth: 1926
Place of birth: Préveza, Greece

Name: Harry Pauly
Date of birth: 1914
Place of birth: Germany

Name: Judith Kàlmàn
Date of birth: August 23, 1927
Place of birth: Erdâbenye, Hungary

Name: Willibald Wohlfahrt
Date of birth: December 15, 1927
Place of birth: Köstenberg-Velden, Austria

Name: Helga Leeser

Date of birth: 1928

Place of birth: Münster, Germany

Name: Irene Freund

Date of birth: October 15, 1930

Place of birth: Mannheim, Germany

Name: Lore Heumann

Date of birth: March 29, 1931

Place of birth: Hellenthal, Germany

Name: Liane Reif

Date of birth: November 14, 1934

Place of birth: Vienna, Austria

Name: Julian Noga

Date of birth: July 31, 1921

Place of birth: Skrzynka, Poland

Name: Helene Lebel

Date of birth: September 15, 1911

Place of birth: Vienna, Austria

Place of birth: Majlech Kisielnicki

Date of birth: August 18, 1920

Place of birth: Kaľuszyn, Poland

Name: Sándor Braun

Date of birth: July 13, 1930

Place of birth: Cristuru-Secuiesc, Romania

Name: Preben Munch-Nielsen

Date of birth: June 13, 1926

Place of birth: Snekkersten, Denmark

Name: Margot Heumann

Date of birth: February 17, 1928

Place of birth: Hellenthal, Germany

Next page: Hitler Youth responding to the pageantry at a gathering of the Nazi Party Congress, Nuremberg, Germany, November 1938. *Hugh Jaeger, Life magazine, Time Warner Inc., New York, N.Y.*

PART ONE
Nazi Germany

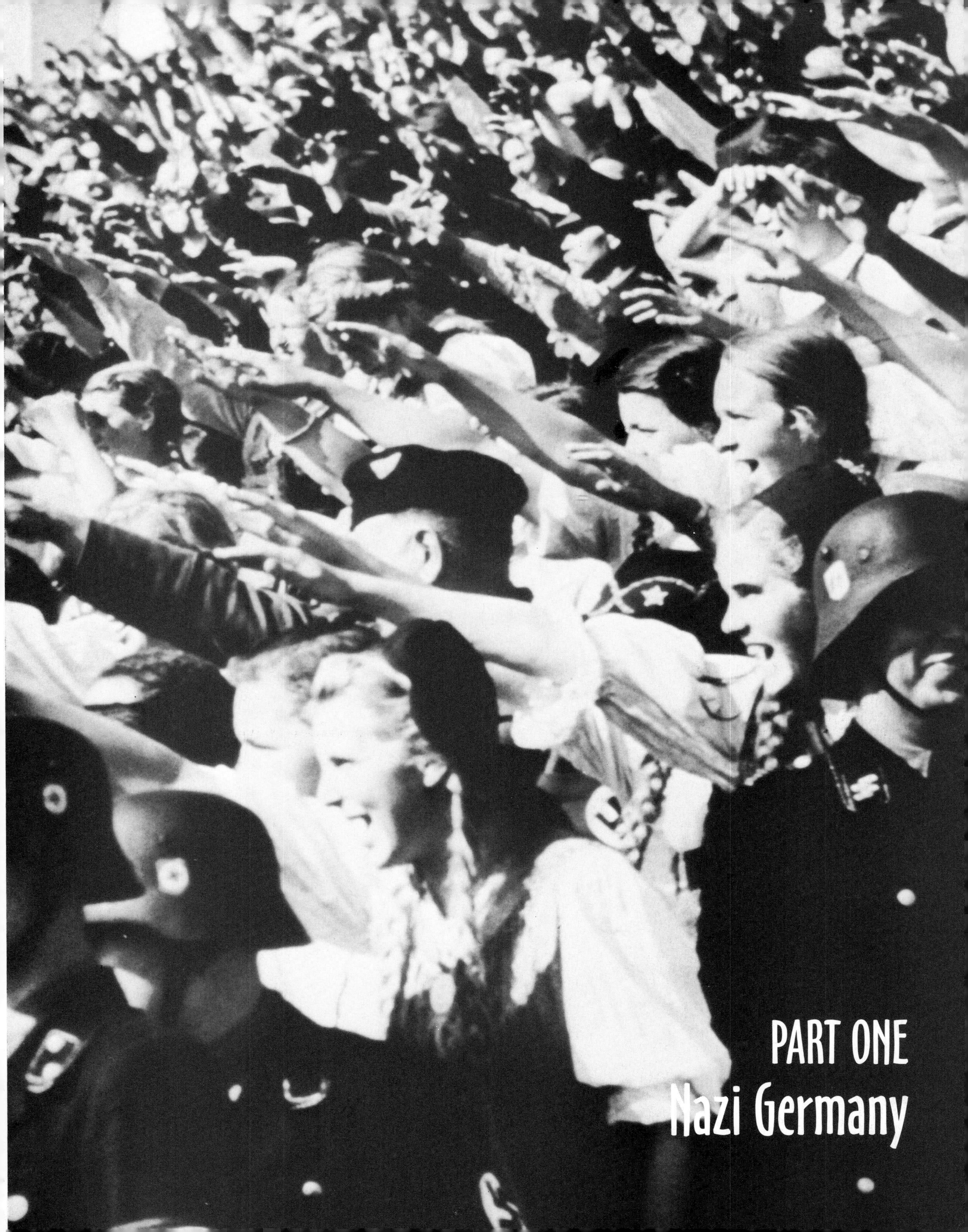

Jewish Life in Europe Before the Holocaust

In 1933, Idzia Pienknawiesz was 13 years old. She lived with her family in Kałuszyn, a mainly Jewish suburb of Warsaw, Poland. Idzia's father owned a liquor store. On summer evenings, Idzia liked to stroll down the main street and visit the candy shop with her friends Majlech Kisielnicki and Masza Tenenbaum. Sometimes they played dominoes or checkers; they also loved to discuss politics.

When the Nazis came to power in Germany in 1933, Jews were living in every country of Europe. A total of roughly nine million Jews lived in the twenty-one countries that would be occupied by Germany during World War II. By the end of the war, two out of every three of these Jews would be dead, and European Jewish life would be changed forever.

In 1933 the largest Jewish populations were concentrated in Eastern Europe, including Poland, the Soviet Union, Hungary, and Romania. Many of the Jews of Eastern Europe lived in predominantly Jewish towns or villages, called *shtetls*. The Jews lived a separate life as a minority within the culture of the majority. They spoke their own language, Yiddish, which combines elements of German and Hebrew. They read Yiddish books, and attended Yiddish theater and movies. Although many younger Jews in larger towns were beginning to adopt modern ways and dress, older people often dressed traditionally, the men wearing hats or caps, and the women modestly covering their hair with wigs or kerchiefs.

In comparison, the Jews in Western Europe — Germany, France, Italy, Holland, and Belgium — made up much less of

Barefooted Jewish children playing in the street before September 1, 1939. Pilviskia, Lithuania. *Yad Vashem, Jerusalem, Israel.*

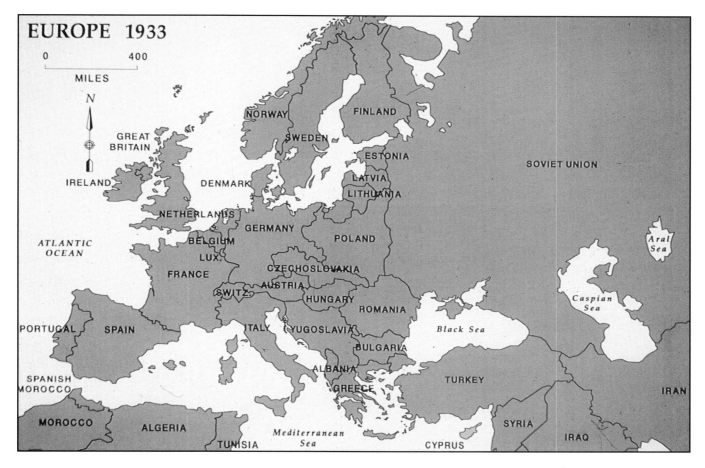

EUROPE 1933

0   400

MILES

N

GREAT
BRITAIN

IRELAND

DENMARK

NETHERLANDS

ATLANTIC
OCEAN

BELGIUM

LUX.

FRANCE

PORTUGAL   SPAIN

SPANISH
MOROCCO

MOROCCO   ALGERIA

NORWAY

SWEDEN

FINLAND

ESTONIA

LATVIA

LITHUANIA

GERMANY

POLAND

SOVIET UNION

Aral
Sea

CZECHOSLOVAKIA

AUSTRIA

SWITZ.

HUNGARY

ROMANIA

Caspian
Sea

ITALY

YUGOSLAVIA

BULGARIA

Black Sea

ALBANIA

GREECE

TURKEY

IRAN

SYRIA

TUNISIA

Mediterranean
Sea

CYPRUS

IRAQ

Map of Europe, 1933. USHMM.

 In 1933, *Barbara Ledermann was 8 years old. She lived with her 5-year-old sister, Susanne, and their parents in the German capital of Berlin, where her father worked as a lawyer. Barbara liked to play with her sister on the porch of their home and enjoyed visiting the city's zoo, parks, and art museums with her family.*

the population and tended to adopt the culture of their non-Jewish neighbors. They dressed and talked like their countrymen, and traditional religious practices and Yiddish culture played a less important part in their lives. They tended to have had more formal education than Eastern European Jews and live in towns or cities.

Jews could be found in all walks of life, as farmers, tailors, seamstresses, factory hands, accountants, doctors, teachers, and small-business owners. Some families were wealthy; many more were poor. Many children ended their schooling early to work in a craft or trade; others looked forward to continuing their education at the university level. Still, whatever their differences, they were the same in one respect: by the 1930s, with the rise of the Nazis to power in Germany, they all became potential victims, and their lives were forever changed.

Jewish youth living in the various countries of Europe included:

Judith Kàlmàn was 6 years old in 1933. An only child, she lived with her parents in Hatvan, a town northeast of Budapest, Hungary. Judith's father worked in the office of his brother's business. On summer vacations, Judith loved to visit her grandparents, who lived in the highlands of northeastern Hungary. She enjoyed playing in the large garden and fruit orchards.

Joseph Gani was 7 years old in 1933. He lived with his family in Préveza, a small Greek town on the Ionian seashore. Joseph's father had a small textile shop. The boy attended public school and every week also received a few hours' religious instruction with the local rabbi. In his free time, Joseph liked to play soccer and other sports.

Sándor Braun was 3 years old in 1933. He lived with his parents and brothers and sisters in Cristuru-Sexuiesc, a small Romanian city. Before his fourth birthday, "Sanyi" wandered away from his babysitter during an outing in the woods. Some roaming Gypsies found him and cared for him and, three days later, returned him to his distraught parents. Having enjoyed the Gypsy music, Sanyi got his wish when his parents presented him with a small violin and provided him with music lessons.

Majlech Kisielnicki (*standing*) and his friends boating, near Warsaw, Poland, before the war. *Donated by Michael Kishel.* USHMM.

Rosetta and Donata Forti on their bicycles beside their brother, Alfredo. Florence, Italy, 1937. *Beth Hatefutsoth Museum of the Jewish Diaspora, Tel Aviv, Israel.*

Antisemitism

Antisemitism is a starting place for trying to understand the tragedy that would befall Barbara Ledermann, Idzia Pienknawiesz, and countless people like them during the Holocaust.

Throughout history Jews have faced prejudice and discrimination, known as antisemitism. Driven from the land now called Israel by the Romans nearly two thousand years ago, they spread throughout the globe and tried to retain their unique beliefs and culture while living as a minority. In some countries Jews were welcomed, and they enjoyed long periods of peace with their neighbors. In European societies where the population was primarily Christian, Jews found themselves increasingly isolated as outsiders. Jews do not share the Christian belief that Jesus is the Son of God, and many Christians considered this refusal to accept Jesus' divinity as arrogant. For centuries the Church taught that Jews were responsible for Jesus' death, not recognizing, as most historians do today, that Jesus was executed by the Roman government because officials viewed him as a political threat to their rule. Added to religious conflicts were economic ones. Rulers placed restrictions on Jews, barring them from holding certain jobs and from owning land. At the same time, since the early Church did not permit *usury* (lending money at interest), Jews came to fill the vital (but unpopular) role of moneylenders for the Christian majority. In more desperate times, Jews became scapegoats for many problems people suffered. For example, they were blamed for causing the "Black Death," the plague that killed thousands of people throughout Europe during the Middle Ages. In Spain in the 1400s, Jews were forced to convert to Christianity, leave the country, or be executed. In Russia and Poland in the late 1800s the government organized or did not prevent violent attacks on Jewish neighborhoods, called *pogroms*, in which mobs murdered Jews and looted their homes and stores.

As ideas of political equality and freedom spread in western Europe during the 1800s, Jews became almost equal citizens under the law. At the same time, however, new forms of antisemitism emerged. European leaders who wanted to establish colonies in Africa and Asia argued that whites were superior to other races and therefore had to spread and take over the "weaker" and "less civilized" races. Some writers applied this argument to Jews, too, mistakenly defining Jews as a race of people called Semites who shared common blood and physical features.* This kind of racial antisemitism meant that Jews remained Jews by race even if they converted to Christianity. Some politicians began using the idea of racial superiority in their campaigns as a way to get votes. Karl Lueger (1844–1910) was one such politician. He became Mayor of Vienna, Austria, at the end of the century through the use of antisemitism — he appealed to voters by blaming Jews for bad economic times. Lueger was a hero to a young man named Adolf Hitler, who was born in Austria in 1889. Hitler's ideas, including his views of Jews, were shaped during the years he lived in Vienna, where he studied Lueger's tactics and the antisemitic newspapers and pamphlets that multiplied during Lueger's long rule.

---

*In fact, Jews are not a race, even by nineteenth-century definitions. There are many Semites who are not Jews, including Arabs, and many Jews, including those who convert to Judaism and their descendants, who are not Semites. Semites, in any case, are simply a branch of the Caucasian (white) race.

Hitler Comes to Power

In the early 1930s, the mood in Germany was grim. The worldwide economic depression had hit the country especially hard, and millions of people were out of work. Still fresh in the minds of many was Germany's humiliating defeat fifteen years earlier during World War I, and Germans lacked confidence in their weak government, known as the Weimar Republic. These conditions provided the chance for the rise of a new leader, Adolf Hitler, and his party, the National Socialist German Workers Party, or Nazis for short. Hitler was a powerful and spellbinding speaker who attracted a wide following of Germans desperate for change. He promised the disenchanted a better life and a new and glorious Germany. The Nazis appealed especially to the unemployed, young people, and members of the lower middle class (small store owners, office employees, craftsmen, farmers). The party's rise to power was rapid. Before the depression struck, the Nazis were practically unknown, winning only 3 percent of the vote to the German parliament, or *Reichstag*. In the 1932 elections, the Nazis won 33 percent of the votes, more than any other party. In January 1933 Hitler was appointed Chancellor, the head of the German government, and many Germans believed that they had found a savior for their nation.

Next page, inset: Portrait of Hitler on propaganda poster captioned "One People, One State, One Leader." USHMM.

Ein Volk, ein Reich, ein Führer!

Chancellor Adolf Hitler waving to crowd on the day he took office. Berlin, Germany, 1935. *Bundesarchiv, Koblenz, Germany.*

The Nazi Terror Begins

In 1933, Wolfgang Munzer was 13 years old, a high school student, living in Berlin. His father was a local leader of the Social Democratic Party, a major party in Germany with many members. Like other Socialists, Mr. Munzer was upset the day Hitler came to power. A few days later, someone slipped a note under the Munzers' door, warning Mr. Munzer that as a political enemy of the Nazis, his life was in danger. The Munzers quickly packed a few belongings and went into hiding. Finally, Mr. Munzer fled Germany and found refuge in Paris. After Wolfgang's mother was hospitalized in Berlin, the teenager ended up in a Jewish orphanage.

Hitler moved quickly to turn Germany into a one-party dictatorship and to organize the police power necessary to enforce Nazi policies. He persuaded his Cabinet to declare a state of emergency and end individual freedoms, including freedom of the press, speech, and assembly. Individuals lost the right of privacy, which meant that officials could read people's mail, listen in on telephone conversations, and search private homes without a warrant.

Hitler also relied on terror to achieve his goals. Lured by the wages, a feeling of comradeship, and the striking uniforms, tens of thousands of young jobless men put on the brown shirts and high leather boots of the Nazi Storm Troopers (*Sturmabteilungen*). Called the SA, these auxiliary policemen took to the streets to beat up and kill some opponents of the Nazi regime. Mere fear of the SA pressured into silence other Germans who did not support the Nazis.

Another important tool of Nazi terror was the Protective Squad (*Schutzstaffel*), or SS, which began as a special guard for Hitler and other party leaders. The black-shirted SS members formed a smaller, elite group whose members also served as auxiliary policemen and, later, as concentration camp guards. Eventually overshadowing the SA in importance, the SS became, after 1934, the private army of the Nazi party.

SS chief Heinrich Himmler also turned the regular (nonparty) police forces into an instrument of terror. He helped forge the powerful Secret State Police (*Geheime Staatspolizei*), or Gestapo; these nonuniformed police used ruthless and cruel methods throughout Germany to identify and arrest political opponents and others who refused to obey laws and policies of the Nazi regime.

In the months after Hitler seized power, the SA and Gestapo agents went from door to door looking for Hitler's enemies. Socialists, Communists, trade union leaders, and others who had spoken out against the Nazi party were arrested, and some were killed. By the middle of 1933, the Nazi party was the only political party, and nearly all organized opposition to the regime had been eliminated. Democracy was dead in Germany.

Many different groups, including the SA and SS, set up hundreds of makeshift "camps" in empty warehouses, factories, and other locations all over Germany where they held political opponents without trial and under conditions of great cruelty. One of these camps was set up on March 20, 1933 at Dachau, in an abandoned munitions factory from World War I. Located near Munich in southwestern Germany, Dachau would become the "model" concentration camp for a vast system of SS camps.

Political opponents being arrested. Berlin, Germany, 1933.
Fédération National des Internées, Résistants, et Partisans, Paris, France.

Inset: Police officer and SS member patrolling the streets. Berlin, Germany, March 5, 1933.
Bundesarchiv, Koblenz, Germany.

Nazi Racism

For years before Hitler became Chancellor, he was obsessed with ideas about race. In his speeches and writings, Hitler spread his beliefs in racial "purity" and in the superiority of the "Germanic race" — what he called an Aryan "master race." He pronounced that his race must remain pure in order to one day take over the world. For Hitler, the ideal "Aryan" was blond, blue-eyed, and tall. When Hitler and the Nazis came to power, these beliefs became the government ideology and were spread in publicly displayed posters, on the radio, in movies, in classrooms, and in newspapers. The Nazis began to put their ideology into practice with the support of those German scientists who believed that the human race could be improved by limiting the reproduction of people considered "inferior."* Beginning in 1933, German physicians were allowed to perform forced sterilizations, operations making it impossible for the victims to have children. Among the targets of this public program were Gypsies, an ethnic minority numbering about 30,000 in Germany, and handicapped individuals, including the mentally ill and people born deaf and blind. Also victimized were about 500 African-German children, the offspring of German mothers and African colonial soldiers in the Allied armies that occupied the German Rhineland region after World War I.

Hitler and other Nazi leaders viewed the Jews not as a religious group, but as a poisonous "race," which "lived off" the other races and weakened them. After Hitler took power, Nazi teachers in school classrooms began to apply the "principles" of racial science. They measured skull size and nose length, and recorded the color of their pupils' hair and eyes to determine whether students belonged to the true "Aryan race." Jewish and Gypsy students were often humiliated in the process.

Joseph Müller was born to Gypsy parents in Bitterfeld, Germany, in 1932. In school he was taunted with insults, became the scapegoat for classroom pranks, and was beaten for "misbehaving" by classmates who were members of Nazi youth groups.

Gad Beck was 10 years old when the Nazis came to power. As one of a small number of Jewish pupils in his school, he quickly became the target of antisemitic comments, such as "Can I sit somewhere else, not next to Gad? He has such stinking Jewish feet." In 1934 Gad's parents enrolled him in a Jewish school. Then, at age 12, he had to quit school because his parents could no longer afford the tuition. He found work as a shop assistant.

---

*The "science" of controlled breeding, called *eugenics*, had many supporters across Europe and the United States in the 1920s and 1930s. Eugenics became a basis for national policies only in Nazi Germany, however.

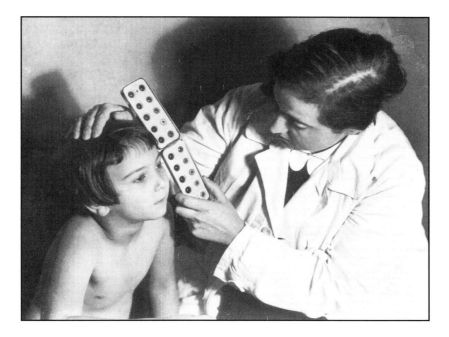

"Scientific" examination of eye color with comparative chart, Berlin, 1936. *Abraham Pisarek Collection, Berlin, Germany.*

Slide used by Dr. Schultz in lectures on genetics and race at the State Academy for Race and Health in Dresden. The slide was captioned: "Mulatto child of a German woman and a Negro of the French Rhineland garrison troops, among her German classmates." Munich, Germany, c. 1936. *Library of Congress, Washington, D.C.*

The Boycott of Jewish Businesses

In 1933, about 600,000 Jews lived in Germany, less than one percent of the total population. Most Jews in Germany were proud to be Germans, citizens of a country that had produced many great poets, writers, musicians, and artists. More than 100,000 German Jews had served in the German army during World War I, and many were decorated for bravery.

Jews held important positions in government and taught in Germany's great universities. Of the thirty-eight Nobel Prizes won by German writers and scientists between 1905 and 1936, fourteen went to Jews. Marriage between Jews and non-Jews was becoming more common. Although German Jews continued to encounter some discrimination in their social lives and professional careers, most were confident of their future as Germans. They spoke the German language and regarded Germany as their home.

When the Nazis came to power, the lives of German Jews changed drastically. On April 1, 1933, the Nazis carried out the first nationwide, planned action against them: a boycott of Jewish businesses. Nazi spokesmen claimed the boycott was an act of revenge against both German Jews and foreigners, including U.S. and English journalists, who had criticized the Nazi regime. On the day of the boycott, storm troopers stood menacingly in front of Jewish-owned shops. The six-pointed "Star of David" was painted in yellow and black across thousands of doors and windows. Signs were posted saying "Don't Buy from Jews" and "The Jews Are Our Misfortune."

The boycott was not very successful and lasted just a day, but it marked the beginning of a nationwide campaign by the Nazi party against the entire German Jewish population. A week later, the government passed a law restricting employment in the civil service to "Aryans." Jewish government workers, including teachers in public schools and universities were fired.

Soon after the Nazis came to power, it became illegal for Jewish lawyers to have non-Jewish clients. The law practice of Barbara Ledermann's father quickly folded. Mr. Ledermann decided to move his family to the Netherlands. Barbara and her sister, Susanne, quickly made friends in their new neighborhood in Amsterdam. Some of their friends, including Margot and Anne Frank, were also Jewish refugees from Germany.

As a passerby looks on, an SA
member (*left*) and SS man
cover a display window with
signs urging German citizens
not to buy from Jews. Berlin,
Germany, April 1933.
Bundesarchiv, Koblenz, Germany.

Nazi Propaganda and Censorship

Once they succeeded in ending democracy and turning Germany into a one-party dictatorship, the Nazis orchestrated a massive propaganda campaign to win the loyalty and cooperation of Germans. The Nazi Propaganda Ministry, directed by Dr. Joseph Goebbels, took control of all forms of communication in Germany: newspapers, magazines, books, public meetings, and rallies, art, music, movies, and radio. Viewpoints in any way threatening to Nazi beliefs or to the regime were censored or eliminated from all media.

During the spring of 1933, Nazi student organizations, professors, and librarians made up long lists of books they thought should not be read by Germans. Then, on the night of May 10, 1933, Nazis raided libraries and bookstores across Germany. They marched by torchlight in nighttime parades, sang chants, and threw books into huge bonfires. On that night more than 25,000 books were burned. Some were works of Jewish writers, including Albert Einstein and Sigmund Freud. Most of the books were by non-Jewish writers, including such famous Americans as Jack London, Ernest Hemingway, and Sinclair Lewis, whose ideas the Nazis viewed as different from their own and therefore not to be read.

The Nazi censors also burned the books of Helen Keller, who had overcome her deafness and blindness to become a respected writer; told of the book burnings, she responded: "Tyranny cannot defeat the power of ideas." Hundreds of thousands of people in the United States protested the book burnings, a clear violation of freedom of speech, in public rallies in New York, Philadelphia, Chicago, and St. Louis.

Schools also played an important role in spreading Nazi ideas. While some books were removed from classrooms by censors, other textbooks, newly written, were brought in to teach students a blind obedience to the party, love for Hitler, and antisemitism. After-school meetings of the Hitler Youth and the League of German Girls trained children to be faithful to the Nazi party. In school and out, young people celebrated such occasions as Hitler's birthday and the anniversary of his taking power.

German children poring over an antisemitic schoolbook, *The Poisonous Mushroom*, which aimed to instill hatred of Jews in the very young. Germany, c. 1938. *Stadt Nürnberg, Nuremberg, Germany.*

The Nuremberg Race Laws

At the annual party rally held in Nuremberg in 1935, the Nazis announced new laws that made Jews second-class citizens by taking away voting and other rights. They were prohibited from marrying or having sexual relations with persons of "German or related blood."

The Nuremberg Laws, as they became known, did not define "Jew" as someone with particular religious beliefs. Instead, anyone who had three or four Jewish grandparents was defined as a Jew, regardless of whether that individual identified himself or herself as a Jew or belonged to the Jewish religious community. Many Germans who had not practiced Judaism for years found themselves caught in the grip of Nazi terror. Even people with Jewish grandparents who had converted to Christianity were defined as Jews.

For a brief period after Nuremberg, in the weeks before and during the 1936 Olympic Games held in Berlin, the Nazi regime actually softened its anti-Jewish attacks and even removed some of the signs saying "Jews Unwelcome" from public places. Hitler did not want international criticism of his government to lead to the Games being moved to another country. Such a loss would have been a serious blow to German prestige.

After the Olympic Games (in which the Nazis did not allow German Jewish athletes to participate), the Nazis again stepped up the persecution of German Jews. In 1937 and 1938, the government set out to impoverish Jews by requiring them to register their property and then by "Aryanizing" Jewish businesses. This meant that Jewish workers and managers were dismissed, and the ownership of most Jewish businesses was taken over by Germans who bought them at bargain prices fixed by Nazis. Jewish doctors were forbidden to treat non-Jews, and Jewish lawyers were not permitted to practice law.

Like everyone in Germany, Jews were required to carry identity cards, but the government added special identifying marks to theirs: a red "J" stamped on them and new middle names — "Israel" for males, "Sara" for females. Such cards allowed the police to identify Jews easily.

Jewish woman on a park bench
marked "For Jews Only."
Annexed Austria, 1938.
Keystone/Hulton-Deutsch, London,
England.

"Enemies of the State"

At 15, Harry Pauly began acting in minor roles in the theater. He spent most of his time with other actors, both at the theater and in nightclubs. Harry was 18 when the Nazis came to power. In 1936 he was arrested for being a homosexual and imprisoned in a camp at Neusustrum, where he was forced to work in the marshes 12 hours a day. He was released after 15 months.

Willibald Wohlfahrt lived in Austria, in a beautiful area near lakes and mountains. His parents were active in Jehovah's Witness missionary work, even though the Austrian government was opposed to the teachings of this group. In 1938 the Nazis took over Austria. Willibald was 11 years old when he saw his father arrested on September 1, 1939, for refusing to enter military service. Three months later, having refused to deny his religious beliefs to save his life, Mr. Wohlfahrt was executed.

Although Jews were the main target of Nazi hatred, they were not the only group persecuted. Other individuals and groups were considered "undesirable" and "enemies of the state." Once the voices of political opponents, like Wolfgang Munzer's father, were silenced, the Nazis stepped up their terror against other "outsiders."

Like Jews, Gypsies were targeted by the Nazis as "non-Aryans" and racial "inferiors." Gypsies belonged to an ethnic group called Roma and Sinti. They had been in Germany since the 1400s and had faced prejudice there for centuries. They had also been victims of official discrimination long before 1933. Under the Nazis, Gypsy families in major cities were rounded up, fingerprinted and photographed, and forced to live in special camps under police guard.

Jehovah's Witnesses, members of a small Christian sect, were victimized not for reasons of race but because of their beliefs. Witnesses' beliefs prohibited them from entering the army or showing obedience to any government by saluting the flag or, in Nazi Germany, raising their arms in the "Heil Hitler" salute. Soon after Hitler took power, Witnesses were sent to concentration camps. Those who remained at large lost their jobs, unemployment and social welfare benefits, and all civil rights. The Witnesses, nevertheless, continued to meet, to preach, and to distribute religious pamphlets.

Homosexuals were victimized by the Nazis for reasons of behavior. The Nazis viewed homosexual relations as "abnormal" and "unmanly" behavior which, by not producing babies, threatened Nazi policies encouraging the reproduction of "Aryans." Soon after Hitler took office, the storm troopers began raids against homosexual clubs. Many homosexuals were arrested and imprisoned in concentration camps. Dozens of teenagers were in this group.

"Enemy of the state." Gypsy
girl interned at Camp Halle,
Germany, 1938-1940.
Bundesarchiv, Koblenz, Germany.

Locating the Victims

In 1939 the German government conducted a census of all persons living in Germany. Census takers recorded each person's age, sex, residence, profession, religion, and marital status, and for the first time, they also listed the person's race as traced through his or her parents and grandparents. This information was later punched into coded cards by thousands of clerks.

The cards were sorted and counted by the Hollerith machine, an early version of the modern computer. The Hollerith was invented in 1884 by a German-American engineer, Herman Hollerith. The machine was used in the United States and by most European governments for processing census data in the late 1800s and early 1900s. The Holleriths used by the Germans were developed by a German branch of the American company later known as International Business Machines (IBM).

The information from the 1939 census helped Nazi official Adolf Eichmann to create the Jewish Registry, containing detailed information on all Jews living in Germany. The Registry also recorded the names of Jews in Austria and the Sudetenland of western Czechoslovakia, which were occupied by German troops in 1938 and 1939 and made part of the Reich (German empire). Nazi racial ideology and policies did not stop at Germany's borders.

Technology and information that were under other circumstances helpful tools became, under the Nazi regime, a means of locating victims.

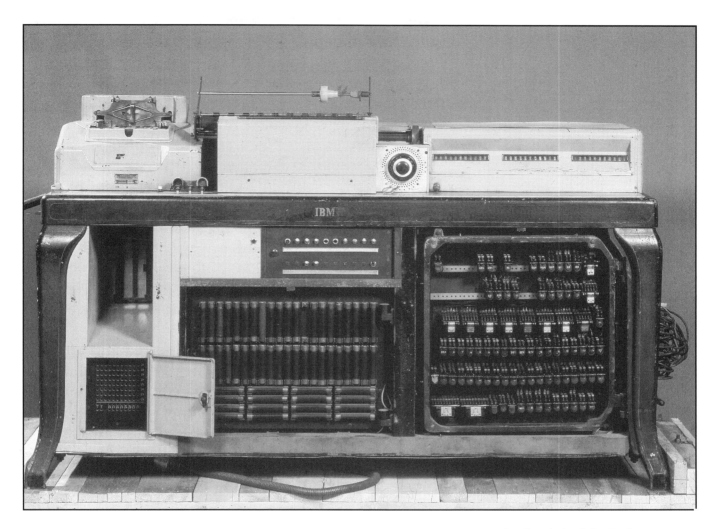

Technology helped the Nazi regime locate its victims. The Hollerith machine was used to process quickly racial and other data gathered for large numbers of people. *Donated by the Museum für Verkehr und Technik, Berlin, Germany. Photo USHMM.*

"Night of Broken Glass"

In 1938, Helga Leeser was 8 years old and living in the small town of Dülmen in western Germany. On the night of November 9, Nazis from a nearby city vandalized her town's Jewish properties. Her father raced downstairs and was arrested; four days later, he committed suicide in his prison cell. Her mother regained her Dutch citizenship and emigrated to the Netherlands. With her grandfather's help, Helga and her sister joined their mother.

In 1938, Irene Freund was 8 years old and living in the industrial city of Mannheim. When the Nazis forced Jewish children out of public schools, she began attending a Jewish school. After the Nazis burned her school, her older brother left for safety in Britain. She remained in Germany, as she was too young to go with him.

On the night of November 9, 1938, violence against Jews broke out across the Reich. It appeared to be unplanned, set off by Germans' anger over the assassination of a German official in Paris at the hands of a Jewish teenager. In fact, Goebbels and other Nazis carefully organized the pogroms. In two days, over one thousand synagogues were burned, seven thousand Jewish businesses were trashed and looted, dozens of Jewish people were killed, and Jewish cemeteries, hospitals, schools, and homes were looted while police and fire brigades stood by, doing nothing. The pogroms became known as *Kristallnacht*, the "Night of Broken Glass," for the shattered glass from store windows that littered the streets.

The morning after the pogroms thirty thousand German Jewish men were arrested for the "crime" of being Jewish and sent to concentration camps, where hundreds of them perished. Some Jewish women were also arrested and sent to local jails. Businesses owned by Jews were not allowed to reopen unless they were managed by non-Jews. Curfews were placed on Jews, limiting the hours of the day they could leave their homes.

After the Night of Broken Glass, life was even more difficult for German and Austrian Jewish children and teenagers. Already barred from entering museums, public playgrounds, and swimming pools, now they were expelled from the public schools. Jewish youngsters, like their parents, were totally segregated in Germany. In despair, many Jewish adults committed suicide. Most families tried desperately to leave.

 Lore Heumann was 7 years old in 1938 when she and her 10-year-old sister, Margot, were expelled from school in Bielefeld, Germany. One day they were suddenly kicked out of class. Not understanding why, they stood outside, crying. Then they walked home. After this, their parents sent them to a Jewish school, where they had teachers who had been kicked out of the schools by the Nazis several years earlier.

Broken glass of shops vandalized by anti-Jewish rioters. Berlin, Germany, November 10, 1938. *Rijksinstituut voor Oorlogsdokumentatie, Amsterdam, Netherlands.*

Jewish children in annexed Austria in class formed after the pupils were expelled from public schools. Graz, Austria, 1938. *Gift of Walter Berman. Yaffa Eliach Collection, Museum of Jewish Heritage, New York, N.Y.*

The Evian Conference

Between 1933 and 1941, the Nazis aimed to make Germany *Judenrein* (cleansed of Jews) by making life so difficult for them that they would be forced to leave the country. By 1938, about 150,000 German Jews, one in four, had already fled the country. After Germany annexed Austria in March 1938, however, an additional 185,000 Jews were brought under Nazi rule. Many Jews were unable to find countries willing to take them in.

Many German and Austrian Jews tried to go to the United States but could not obtain the papers (visas) needed to enter. Even though news of the violent pogroms of November 1938 was widely reported, Americans remained reluctant to welcome Jewish refugees. In the midst of the Great Depression, many Americans believed that refugees would compete with them for jobs and overburden social programs set up to assist the needy.

Congress had set immigration quotas in 1924 that limited the number of immigrants and discriminated against groups considered racially and ethnically undesirable. These quotas remained in place even after President Roosevelt, responding to mounting political pressure, called for an international conference to address the refugee problem.

Hotel Royale at Evian, where delegates to the conference on refugees enjoyed all the pleasures the luxurious spa resort had to offer. Evian-les-Bains, France, July 1938. *National Archives, Washington, D.C.*

Political cartoon on the Evian Conference. *New York Times*, July 3, 1938. *New York Public Library*, New York, N.Y.

In the summer of 1938, delegates from thirty-two countries met at the French resort of Evian. Roosevelt chose not to send a high-level official, such as the Secretary of State, to Evian; instead, Myron C. Taylor, a businessman and close friend of Roosevelt's, represented the U.S. at the conference. During the nine-day meeting, delegate after delegate rose to express sympathy for the refugees. But most countries, including the United States and Britain, offered excuses for not letting in more refugees.

Responding to Evian, the German government was able to state with great pleasure how "astounding" it was that foreign countries criticized Germany for their treatment of the Jews, but none of them wanted to open the doors to them when "the opportunity offer[ed]."

Even efforts by some Americans to rescue children failed: the Wagner-Rogers bill, an effort to admit 20,000 endangered Jewish refugee children, was not supported by the Senate in 1939 and 1940. Widespread racial prejudices among Americans — including antisemitic attitudes held by the U.S. State Department officials — played a part in the failure to admit more refugees.

27

Voyage of the St. Louis

Liane Reif was living in Vienna when German troops entered Austria in 1938. Her father, a dentist, was forced to end his practice, and soon after, he was found dead, a probable suicide. Liane was 5 years old in May 1939 when her mother booked passage on the St. Louis. After the ship was forced to return to Europe, Liane, her brother, and her mother disembarked in the French city of Boulogne.

The voyage of the SS St. Louis, a German ocean liner, dramatically highlights the difficulties faced by many people trying to escape Nazi terror. In May 1939, 936 passengers, all but six of them Jews, left Hamburg, Germany, en route to Cuba. Most of them planned eventually to emigrate to the United States and were on the waiting list for admission. All passengers held visas permitting them entry to Cuba, but when the St. Louis reached the port of Havana, the President of Cuba refused to honor the visas.

After the ship left the Havana harbor, it sailed so close to the Florida coast that the passengers could see the lights of Miami. The captain appealed for help, but in vain. U.S. Coast Guard ships patrolled the waters to make sure that no one jumped to freedom and did not allow the ship to dock in the U.S. The St. Louis turned back to Europe. Belgium, Holland, England, and France admitted the passengers. But within months, the Germans overran western Europe. Except for the 288 passengers who got off the ship in England, most of the people aboard the St. Louis perished in the Holocaust.

Jewish refugee children enjoying festivities aboard the SS St. Louis, headed for Cuba, where they expected to land. May 1939. *Photo donated by Henry Gallant* (the boy standing in the center and blowing a horn). USHMM.

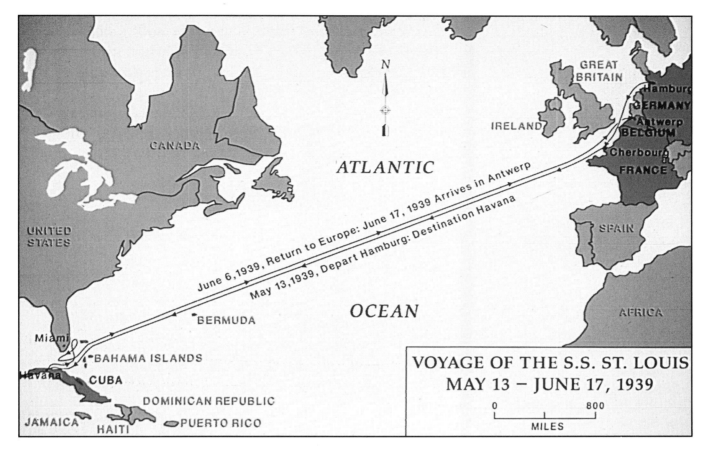

Map labels:

CANADA

ATLANTIC

GREAT BRITAIN

IRELAND

Hamburg
GERMANY
Antwerp
BELGIUM
Cherbourg
FRANCE

UNITED STATES

SPAIN

June 6, 1939, Return to Europe: June 17, 1939 Arrives in Antwerp

May 13, 1939, Depart Hamburg: Destination Havana

OCEAN

AFRICA

BERMUDA

Miami

BAHAMA ISLANDS

Havana   CUBA

DOMINICAN REPUBLIC

JAMAICA   HAITI   PUERTO RICO

VOYAGE OF THE S.S. ST. LOUIS
MAY 13 – JUNE 17, 1939

0   800
MILES

USHMM.

The War Begins

By the late 1930s, Hitler had put together one of the most powerful war machines Europe had ever seen. The *Führer*, as the German leader was called, had grand visions of German domination of Europe. Austria had been added to the Reich in March 1938 and the Sudetenland in western Czechoslovakia a year later. Then, on September 1, 1939, Germany invaded neighboring Poland. World War II had begun.

Within days, the Polish army was destroyed and the Germans began their campaign to destroy Polish culture and to enslave the Polish people. The Nazis viewed the Poles as "subhumans." They wanted to turn them into slaves to serve German masters. Killing Polish leaders was the first step. German soldiers carried out massacres of university professors, artists, teachers, writers, politicians, and many Catholic priests. The second step was to allow no Pole to continue schooling beyond the fourth grade. The primary focus of Polish education was to teach Poles to obey the Germans. To create new living space for the "superior Germanic race," large segments of the Polish population were resettled, and German families moved into the emptied lands.

The Nazis also "kidnapped" as many as 50,000 Polish children from their parents and took them to Germany to be adopted by German families. Chosen were children whose physical appearance most fit the Nazi notion of a "master race" — blond hair, blue eyes, fair skin. Many of these children were later rejected and sent to special children's camps, where they died of starvation or disease.

In 1939, Julian Noga, a Polish Catholic, was 18 years old and working as a dishwasher in the town of Tarnów in southern Poland. After the German invasion, Julian returned home to the village of Skrzynka. There he was betrayed for hiding a rifle abandoned by a retreating Polish soldier. He was deported to Austria to do farm labor for a rich landowner near Linz. On the farm he and the landowner's daughter, Frieda, fell in love. Her father objected, but the couple continued to meet secretly even though the Nazi regime forbade relations between Poles and Germans. The Gestapo warned Julian that if he continued to see Frieda, he would be hanged. He was reassigned to another farm, but they continued to see one another.

Hitler and other high German officers watch the long lines of soldiers marching through Poland after Germany invaded the country on September 1, 1939. AP/*Wide World Photos, Inc., New York, N.Y.*

Execution of Piotr Sosnowski, a Polish priest, in a forested region where 12,000 civilians were shot between November 1939 and April 1944. Piasnica, Poland, c. 1939. *Main Commission for the Investigation of Nazi War Crimes in Poland, Warsaw, Poland.*

The Murder of the Handicapped

Helene Lebel, raised as a Catholic in Vienna, Austria, first showed signs of mental illness when she was 19. Her condition worsened until she had to give up her law studies and her job as a legal secretary. In 1936 she was diagnosed as a schizophrenic, and was placed in Vienna's Steinhof Psychiatric Hospital. Two years later, the Germans annexed Austria to Germany. Helene's condition had improved at Steinhof, and her parents were led to believe that she would soon be moved to a hospital in a nearby town. In fact, Helene was tranferred to a former prison in Brandenburg, Germany. There she was undressed, subjected to a physical examination, and then led into a shower room, where she was murdered with a deadly gas.

Wartime, Hitler suggested, "was the best time for the elimination of the incurably ill." Many Germans did not want to be reminded of individuals who did not measure up to their concept of a "master race." The physically and mentally handicapped were viewed as "useless" to society, a threat to Aryan genetic purity, and, ultimately, unworthy of life. At the beginning of World War II, individuals who were mentally retarded, physically handicapped, or mentally ill were targeted for murder in what the Nazis called the "T-4," or "euthanasia," program.*

The euthanasia program required the cooperation of many German doctors, who reviewed the medical files of patients in institutions to determine which handicapped or mentally ill individuals should be killed. The doctors also supervised the actual killings. Doomed patients were transferred to six institutions in Germany and Austria, where they were killed in specially constructed gas chambers. Handicapped infants and small children were also killed by injection with a deadly dose of drugs or by starvation. The bodies of the victims were burned in large ovens called *crematoria.*

Despite public protests in 1941, the Nazi leadership continued this program in secret throughout the war. More than 200,000 handicapped people were murdered between 1940 and 1945.

The T-4 program became the model for the mass murder of Jews, Gypsies, and others in camps equipped with gas chambers that the Nazis would open in 1941 and 1942. The program also served as a training ground for SS members who manned these camps.

---

* "T-4" refers to the Berlin address, Tiergartenstrasse 4, of the program's headquarters. The Germans twisted the meaning of "euthanasia" to cover up murder; the term usually refers to the practice of killing persons who are hopelessly sick for reasons of mercy.

This castle, in Hartheim,
Austria, was one of the sites
for the "euthanasia" program.
Mentally and physically
disabled persons were
murdered here by lethal
injection and gassing.
Hartheim, Austria, 1934–1945.
Donated by Andras Tsagatakis.
USHMM.

Next page: "Selection" of
Hungarian Jews at Auschwitz.
Most in the group are chosen
to be killed immediately in the
gas chambers. Auschwitz,
Poland, spring 1944. *Yad
Vashem, Jerusalem, Israel.*

PART TWO
The "Final Solution"

Germans Occupy Western Europe

In 1937, when Wolfgang Munzer was 17, he moved to Paris to join his father, who had fled Germany a few years earlier. Six years later, Wolfgang was living in the southern French city of Nice, where his father and stepmother ran a lending library that specialized in books banned by the Nazis. In March 1944, the Nazis transported 24-year-old Wolfgang and his parents to the Drancy transit camp near Paris.

When Susanne Ledermann was 15, she and her sister, Barbara, were forced to enroll in a Jewish school soon after the Germans occupied Amsterdam. In June 1943, Susanne and her parents were taken to the Westerbork transit camp in northeastern Netherlands.

By the middle of 1940, Germany had defeated France, Belgium, Luxembourg, Holland, Denmark, and Norway in the war. Italy joined the German side, as did Romania and Hungary. Much of Europe was now under the domination of Nazi Germany. The Germans moved quickly against the Jews in the conquered countries. Jewish adults lost their jobs, and Jewish students were expelled from public schools. Jews almost everywhere under Nazi rule were forced to purchase and wear a six-pointed Star of David whenever they appeared in public. The yellow or blue star was worn on an armband or pinned on a shirt or coat.

German Jews who had fled Germany to neighboring France, Belgium, or Holland in the 1930s were once again caught in the Nazi net. Some people managed to cross the French border into Spain, make their way via Spain into Portugal, and eventually find refuge overseas. Others went into hiding or changed their identities, trying, for example, to pass as Christians. Tens of thousands of Jews failed to escape and, beginning in the summer of 1942, were arrested, taken to transit camps, and then transported by train or truck eastward to Auschwitz or other Nazi camps, where most of them were murdered (see pages 52–57).

A group of Dutch children talking with a Jewish child through the fence of the Jewish quarter in Amsterdam, sealed off by the Germans in February 1941. Amsterdam, Netherlands, 1941-1943. *Rijks Instituut voor Oorlogsdocumentatie, Amersterdam, Netherlands.*

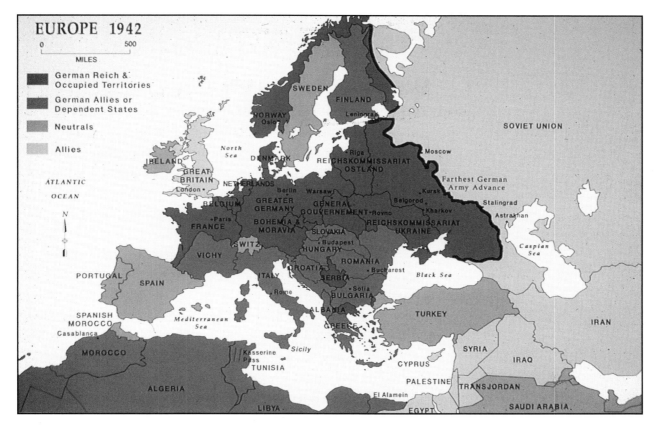

EUROPE 1942

0   500
MILES

- German Reich & Occupied Territories
- German Allies or Dependent States
- Neutrals
- Allies

Map of Europe, 1942. USHMM

Barbara Ledermann was 17 when she obtained false identification papers and remained in hiding with the help of her boyfriend, Manfred, in Amsterdam.

When Helga Leeser was 14, she and her mother and sister avoided being taken from Holland to a Nazi camp by getting false papers saying they were Dutch Christians. A Dutch couple in Rotterdam hid them in their flat, just two blocks from the police station. Because Helga was Jewish-looking, she had to stay inside all the time. She spent her time reading and studying and listening to the radio. Helga's family had problems obtaining food because, like other people in hiding, they did not have the legal ration coupons they needed to buy it. They were reduced to eating mainly sugar beets.

In 1941, Liane Reif was 7 years old. She and her mother, who earlier had found refuge in France after the SS St. Louis returned to Europe, managed in 1941 to make their way to Portugal. From there, they were lucky to book passage to New York on one of the few passenger ships still crossing the Atlantic during the war.

Ghettos in Eastern Europe

Millions of Jews lived in eastern Europe. After Germany invaded Poland in 1939, more than two million Polish Jews came under German control. After Germany invaded the Soviet Union in June 1941, several million more Jews came under Nazi rule.* The Germans aimed to control this sizable Jewish population by forcing Jews to reside in marked-off sections of towns and cities the Nazis called "ghettos" or "Jewish residential quarters." Altogether, the Germans created more than 400 ghettos in occupied territories. The largest ghetto was in Warsaw, the Polish capital, where almost half a million Jews were confined.

Many ghettos were set up in cities and towns where Jews were already concentrated. Jews as well as some Gypsies were also brought to ghettos from surrounding regions and from western Europe. In October and November 1941, the first group of German and Austrian Jews was transported to ghettos in eastern Europe. The Germans usually marked off the oldest, most run-down sections of cities for the ghettos. They sometimes had to evict non-Jewish residents from the buildings to make room for Jewish families. Many of the ghettos were enclosed by barbed-wire fences or walls, with entrances guarded by local and German police and SS members. During curfew hours at night the residents were forced to stay inside their apartments.

In the Polish cities of Łódź and Warsaw, trolley lines ran through the middle of the ghetto. Rather than reroute the lines, workers fenced them off, and policemen guarded the area to keep the Jews from escaping on the trolley cars. The passengers from outside the ghetto used the cars to get to work on weekdays, and some rode them on Sunday outings just to gawk and sneer at the ghetto prisoners.

---

*In 1939 and 1940, the Soviet Union annexed eastern Poland, the Baltic states (Lithuania, Latvia, Estonia), and Bessarabia and Bukŏvina, territories where over two million Jews lived. After the German invasion of the Soviet Union, these areas fell under Nazi rule as well as the western Soviet Union, where hundreds of thousands of Jews lived. Over a million of these Jews would be murdered by mobile killing squads in 1941 and 1942 (see page 42). Many others were imprisoned in ghettos set up in 1941.

Moving into the ghetto. The Germans confined about 10,000 Jews in this ghetto at Drogobych, USSR (Ukraine). October 1942. *Ullstein Bilderdienst, Berlin, Germany.*

Prisoners of the Łódź ghetto walk across a bridge built to segregate them from trolley car riders below. Łódź, Poland, 1941. *Bundesarchiv, Koblenz, Germany.*

Life in the Ghetto

When she was 20, Idzia Pienknawiesz was living in the ghetto of her hometown of Kałuszyn, Poland. Acting under German orders, the town mayor chose a Jewish Council, which included her father and her friend Majlech's father. They, in turn, chose Majlech, Idzia and some other young adults to work on the ghetto sanitation committee. One of Idzia's jobs was to take women to the one remaining Jewish bathing facility in town so they could wash themselves. Everyone was infested with lice, which multiplied because of the terrible overcrowding that occurred after the Germans "resettled" hundreds of Jews from other towns in Kałuszyn. Lice carried typhus germs, a disease that killed tens of thousands of people imprisoned in Kałuszyn and other ghettos.

Life in the ghettos was usually unbearable. Overcrowding was common. An apartment might have several families living in it. Plumbing broke down, and human waste was thrown in the streets with the garbage. Contagious diseases spread rapidly in such cramped, unsanitary housing. People were always hungry. Germans deliberately tried to starve residents by allowing them to purchase only a small amount of bread, potatoes, and fat. Some residents had some money or valuables they could trade for food smuggled into the ghetto; others were forced to beg or steal to survive. During the long winters, heating fuel was scarce, and many people lacked adequate clothing. People weakened by hunger and exposure to the cold became easy victims of disease; tens of thousands died in the ghettos from illness, starvation, or cold. Some individuals killed themselves to escape their hopeless lives.

Every day children became orphaned, and many had to take care of even younger children. Orphans often lived on the streets, begging for bits of bread from others who had little or nothing to share. Many froze to death in the winter.

In order to survive, children had to be resourceful and make themselves useful. Small children in the Warsaw ghetto sometimes helped smuggle food to their families and friends by crawling through narrow openings in the ghetto wall. They did so at great risk, as smugglers who were caught were severely punished.

Many young people tried to continue their education by attending school classes organized by adults in many ghettos. Since such classes were usually held secretly, in defiance of the Nazis, pupils learned to hide books under their clothes when necessary, to avoid being caught.

Although suffering and death were all around them, children did not stop playing with toys. Some had beloved dolls or trucks they brought into the ghetto with them. Children also made toys, using whatever bits of cloth and wood they could find. In the Łódź ghetto, children turned the tops of empty cigarette boxes into playing cards.

A few months before Lore Heumann turned 11, she was deported with her family to the Theresienstadt ghetto in Czechoslovakia. When the Heumanns arrived at the station, they were met by Lore's thin and sickly looking grandmother, who had been deported there some six months earlier. She told them that Lore's grandfather had died a few weeks earlier, from illness and malnutrition. In the ghetto Lore attended the clandestine classes, but she found it hard to concentrate because she was almost always hungry.

A child beggar accepts money from a woman on the streets of the Warsaw ghetto. Warsaw, Poland, 1941. *Bundesarchiv, Koblenz, Germany.*

Children sitting on the ground in the Łódź ghetto. The stars fixed to their clothing identify them as Jews. Łódź, Poland, 1940–1944. YIVO *Institute for Jewish Research, New York, N.Y.*

The Mobile Killing Squads

After the German army invaded the Soviet Union on June 22, 1941, a new stage in the Holocaust began. Under cover of war and confident of victory, the Germans turned from the forced emigration and imprisonment of Jews to the mass murder of them. Special action squads, or *Einsatzgruppen*, made up of Nazi (SS) units and police, moved with speed on the heels of the advancing German army. Their job was to kill any Jews they could find in the occupied Soviet territory. Some residents of the occupied regions, mostly Ukrainians, Latvians, and Lithuanians, aided these German mobile killing squads by serving as auxiliary police.

The mobile killing units acted swiftly, taking the Jewish population by surprise. The killers entered a town or city and rounded up all Jewish men, women, and children. They also took away many Communist party leaders and Gypsies. Victims were forced to surrender any valuables and remove their clothing, which was later sent for use in Germany. Then the killing squad members marched their victims to open fields and ravines on the outskirts of conquered towns and cities. There they shot them and dumped the bodies into mass graves.

On September 21, 1941, the eve of the Jewish New Year, a mobile killing squad entered Ejszyszki, a small town in what is now Lithuania. The killing squad members herded four thousand Jews from the town and the surrounding region into three synagogues, where they were held for two days without food or water. Then, in two days of killing, Jewish men, women, and children were taken to cemeteries, lined up in front of open pits, and shot to death. Today there are no Jews in Ejszyszki. It was one of hundreds of cities, towns, and shtetls whose Jews were murdered during the Holocaust. The rich culture of most of these Jewish communities was lost forever.

The killing squads murdered more than a million Jews and hundreds of thousands of other innocent people. At Babi Yar, near Kiev, about 34,000 Jews were murdered in two days of shooting. Only a few people in the general population helped their Jewish neighbors escape. Most people were afraid that they, too, might be killed.

The massacres of innocent men, women, and children in Babi Yar and other towns were not the crimes of hoodlums or crazy men. The executioners were "ordinary" men who followed the orders of their commanding officers. Many of the killers had wives and children back in Germany. Propaganda and training had taught many members of the mobile killing squads to view their victims as enemies of Germany. Some killers drank heavily to dull their thoughts and feelings. In addition, when they described their actions they used code words like "special treatment" and "special action" instead of "killing" or "murder" to distance themselves from their terrible crimes.

Execution of Soviet Jews by *Einsatzgruppen*. D. Vinnitsa, USSR, 1942. *Library of Congress, Washington, D.C.*

Photographs of young people taken in Ejszyszki, Lithuania, or surroundings, before the war. People of all ages present in this shtetl on September 21, 1941, were murdered by the *Einsatzgruppen. Yaffa Eliach Shtetl Collection*, USHMM.

The Wannsee Conference and the "Final Solution"

On January 20, 1942, fifteen high-ranking Nazi party and German government leaders gathered for an important meeting. They met in a wealthy section of Berlin at a villa by a lake known as Wannsee. Reinhard Heydrich, who was SS Chief Himmler's head deputy, held the meeting for the purpose of discussing the "final solution to the Jewish question in Europe" with key non-SS government leaders, including the Secretaries of the Foreign Ministry and Justice, whose cooperation was needed.

The "final solution" was the Nazis' code name for the deliberate, carefully planned destruction, or *genocide*, of all European Jews. The Nazis used the vague term "final solution" to hide their policy of mass murder from the rest of the world. In fact, the men at Wannsee talked about methods of killing, about liquidation, about "extermination."

The Wannsee Conference, as it became known to history, did not mark the beginning of the "final solution." The mobile killing squads were already slaughtering Jews in the occupied Soviet Union. Rather, the Wannsee Conference was the place where the "final solution" was formally revealed to non-Nazi leaders who would help arrange for Jews to be transported from all over German-occupied Europe to SS-operated "extermination" camps in Poland. Not one of the men present at Wannsee objected to the announced policy. Never before had a modern state committed itself to the murder of an entire people.

Wannsee villa, where German leaders met on January 20, 1942, to discuss the "final solution." Wannsee, Germany, c. 1922. *Ullstein Bilderdienst, Berlin, Germany.*

SS Lieutenant General Reinhard Heydrich, head of the Reich Security Main Office (RSHA), an enormous police organization that included the Gestapo. Heydrich issued the invitations to the Wannsee Conference and chaired the meetings. Germany. *Sueddeutscher Verlag Bilderdienst, Munich, Germany.*

Deportations

Idzia Pienknawiesz was 22 when she was deported from the Kałuszyn ghetto to the Treblinka extermination camp on December 9, 1942. She was among the last residents of Kałuszyn to be deported. Her parents and 3,000 other Jews had been deported to Treblinka that September. Idzia was one of up to 750,000 Jews who were gassed at Treblinka during the 14 months of the camp's operation.

Idzia's close friend, Majlech Kisielnicki, who was also 22 in 1942, managed to escape the roundup in Kałuszyn for deportation. He fled to Warsaw and bribed a guard to take him into the Warsaw ghetto, where he could stay with some cousins. On January 18, 1943, he was caught up in a roundup in the ghetto and put on a cattle car headed for Treblinka. Although the train was moving quite fast and guards were positioned on its roof, ready to machine-gun escapees, Majlech managed to squeeze through the narrow window and jump from the train without being hurt. He returned to Warsaw.

In the months following the Wannsee Conference, the Nazi regime continued to carry out their plans for the "final solution." Jews were "deported" — transported by trains or trucks to six camps, all located in occupied Poland: Chełmno, Treblinka, Sobibór, Bełżec, Auschwitz-Birkenau, and Majdanek-Lublin.

The Nazis called these six camps "extermination camps." Most of the deportees were immediately murdered in large groups by poisonous gas. The Nazis changed to gassing as their preferred method of mass murder because they saw it as "cleaner" and more "efficient" than shooting. Gassing also spared the killers the emotional stress many mobile killing squad members had felt shooting people face to face. The killing centers were in semi-rural, isolated areas, fairly well hidden from public view. They were located near major railroad lines, allowing trains to transport hundreds of thousands of people to the killing sites.

Many of the victims were deported from nearby ghettos, some as early as December 1941, even before the Wannsee meeting. The SS began in earnest to empty the ghettos, however, in the summer of 1942. In two years' time, more than two million Jews were taken out of the ghettos. By the summer of 1944, few ghettos remained in eastern Europe.

At the same time that ghettos were being emptied, masses of Jews and also Gypsies were transported from the many distant countries occupied or controlled by Germany, including France, Belgium, Holland, Norway, Hungary, Romania, Italy, North Africa, and Greece.

The deportations required the help of many people and all arms of the German government. The victims in Poland were already imprisoned in ghettos and totally under German control. The deportation of Jews from other parts of Europe, however, was a far more complex problem. The German Foreign Ministry succeeded in pressuring most governments of occupied and allied nations to assist the Germans in the deportation of Jews living in their countries.

Deportation of Jewish children from an orphanage in the Łódź ghetto to the Chełmno "extermination" camp. Łódź, Poland, September 1942. *Jewish Historical Institute, Warsaw, Poland.*

 *A few weeks after German troops entered Hungary on March 19, 1944, Judith Kàlmàn, who was then 16, was forced with her mother and hundreds of other Jews into a makeshift ghetto set up in a sugar factory in their hometown. One day, Judith and her mother were taken out of the ghetto to work in the nearby fields. Returning at the end of the day, they were forced to walk on the sides of the road and kiss the filthy ground. On the roadsides, jeering and clapping, Judith's so-called "friends" in the crowd laughed and pointed at her. Soon after, Judith and her mother were deported to Auschwitz-Birkenau. The Kàlmàns were among the 434,351 Hungarian Jews who were deported to Auschwitz-Birkenau between May 15 and July 9, 1944. Most of the Hungarian Jews were gassed immediately after their arrival at Auschwitz-Birkenau.*

 *Susanne Ledermann was 15 when she was deported with her parents on June 20, 1943, from the Westerbork transit camp in Holland to Auschwitz-Birkenau, where they all perished.*

 *Joseph Gani was 18 when he was deported in March 1944 with other Jews from his hometown of Préveza, in Greece, to Auschwitz-Birkenau.*

 *When he was nearly 14, Sándor Braun was deported from Romania to Auschwitz-Birkenau in May 1944.*

On the Train

When he was 24, Wolfgang Munzer and his parents were deported, on March 7, 1944, from the Drancy transit camp in France to Auschwitz-Birkenau. The trip, in a sealed freight car, took four days. Some people on the train did not survive the trip.

When she was 13, Lore Heumann, her 15-year-old sister, Margot, their parents, and their grandmother were deported from the Theresienstadt ghetto to Auschwitz-Birkenau, in May 1944. The trip in the freight car took more than two days. There was barely room to stand, and only a bucket as a toilet. When they arrived in Auschwitz, they had no idea what to expect. Lore's sister Margot, alone, survived.

Most deportees did not know that they were going to their deaths. The Germans were usually very careful to hide the real destination of the trains so that people would not panic or resist. Victims were told that they were being "resettled in the east" or being sent to labor camps.

The train trip sometimes took just a few hours. Sometimes it took days. Some deportees were ticketed as passengers, but ticketed or not, people were most often treated like freight. They were crammed into boxcars until there was no room for anyone to move. Freight cars had no seats, no bathroom facilities, and only slatted openings as windows, so inside it was dark, and the air reeked with the smell of bodies and human waste. The trains were unbearably hot in the summer and freezing cold in the winter. During the trip there was no food except for what people managed to bring along. On the long trips, many people died on the trains of starvation, lack of air, or illness.

When the doors opened upon arrival, the passengers who survived the trip were exhausted and bewildered. Some of them were grateful and relieved, believing that nothing could be worse than the hellish train ride they had endured.

Hungarian Jews arrive at Auschwitz. Auschwitz, Poland, spring 1944. Yad Vashem, Jerusalem, Israel.

Women and children from a
Hungarian transport after its
arrival at Auschwitz-Birkenau.
Auschwitz, Poland, spring
1944. *Yad Vashem, Jerusalem,
Israel.*

At the Killing Centers

After the trains arrived at the camps, guards ordered the deportees to get out and form a line. The victims then went through a selection process. Men were separated from women and children. A Nazi, usually an SS physician, looked quickly at each person to decide if he or she was healthy and strong enough for slave labor. This SS officer then pointed to the left or to the right; victims did not know that individuals were being selected to live or to die. Babies and young children, pregnant women, the elderly, the handicapped, and the sick had little chance of surviving this first selection.

Those who had been selected to die were led to gas chambers. In order to prevent panic, camp guards told the victims that they were going to take showers to rid themselves of lice. The guards instructed them to turn over all their valuables and to undress. Then they were driven naked into the "showers." A guard closed and locked the steel door. In some killing centers, carbon monoxide was piped into the chamber. In others, camp guards threw "Zyklon B" pellets down an air shaft. Zyklon B was a highly poisonous insecticide also used to kill rats and insects.

Usually within minutes after entering the gas chambers, everyone inside was dead from lack of oxygen. Under guard, prisoners were forced to haul the corpses to a nearby room, where they removed hair, gold teeth, and fillings. The bodies were burned in ovens in the crematoria or buried in mass graves.

Many people profited from the pillage of the corpses. Camp guards stole some of the gold. The rest was melted down and deposited in an SS bank account. Private business firms bought and used the hair to make many products, including ship rope and mattresses.

The inside of a gas chamber at Majdanek. From the outside, SS guards were able to observe the killing through the small peephole in the door. *Photo*: USHMM.

Inset: Chalky pellets containing the deadly prussic acid gas sold as "Zyklon B" and used in the gas chambers of Auschwitz-Birkenau and Majdanek. *On loan from the State Museum of Auschwitz, Oświęcim, Poland; State Museum of Majdanek, Lublin, Poland; KZ-Gedenkstätte Sachsenhausen, Germany. Photo: USHMM.*

Auschwitz-Birkenau

Auschwitz-Birkenau was the largest of the Nazi death camps, located near Cracow, Poland. More than one million people lost their lives at this camp, nine out of ten of them Jewish. The four largest gas chambers could each hold 2,000 people at one time.

A sign over the entrance to Auschwitz-Birkenau read *Arbeit Macht Frei*, which means "work makes one free." In the camps, however, the opposite was true. Labor became another form of genocide that the Nazis called "extermination through work."

Victims who were spared immediate death by being selected for labor were systematically stripped of their individual identities. They had their hair shaved off and a registration number tattooed on their left forearm. Men were forced to wear ragged, striped pants and jackets, and women wore work dresses. Both were issued ill-fitting work shoes, sometimes clogs. They had no change of clothing and slept in the same clothes they worked in.

Each day was a struggle for survival under unbearable conditions. Prisoners were housed in primitive barracks that had no windows and were not insulated from the heat or cold. There was no bathroom, only a bucket. Each barrack held about thirty-six wooden bunkbeds, and inmates were squeezed in five or six across on the wooden plank. As many as 500 inmates lodged in a single barrack.

Inmates were always hungry. Food consisted of watery soup

After Wolfgang Munzer arrived at Auschwitz-Birkenau, he went through "selection" and was separated from his parents. He was not in the camp long before he realized his parents had been gassed. He was put to work in a factory run by the Siemens company, which manufactured electrical components.

Barracks at the Birkenau camp, which was part of the large Auschwitz-Birkenau complex. Auschwitz, Poland, February 1945. *Sovfoto*, New York, N.Y.

Roll call (*Appell*). Prisoners are identified by colored triangles and numbers on their chests instead of by their names. At most camps, the day began and ended with roll calls which sometimes lasted for hours, even in freezing rain or snow. Buchenwald, Germany, 1942–1943. *Yad Vashem, Jerusalem, Israel.*

made with rotten vegetables and meat, a few ounces of bread, a bit of margarine, tea, or a bitter drink resembling coffee. Diarrhea was common. People weakened by dehydration and hunger fell easy victim to the contagious diseases that spread through the camp.

Some inmates worked as forced laborers inside the camp, in the kitchen or as barbers, for example. Women often sorted the piles of shoes, clothes, and other prisoner belongings, which would be shipped back to Germany for use there. The storage warehouses at Auschwitz-Birkenau, located near two of the crematoria, were called "Canada," because the Poles regarded that country as a place of great riches. At Auschwitz,

Judith Kàlmàn, who had been selected for slave labor, was unwilling to believe that her mother had been killed in the gas chambers. Judith was taken with 500 other inmates to an airplane factory in Augsburg in southwestern Germany, where she cleared rubble from Allied bombing raids. Three months later she was moved inside the factory, out of the cold and rain, where she worked beside German factory hands. One of them brought Judith and her girlfriend food every morning.

Sándor Braun was 14 when he was sent from Auschwitz to Dachau. One day a camp guard, promising extra food, entered his barracks holding a violin, and asked if anyone could play. Sándor and two others volunteered. The first two prisoners did not please the guard, and they were both killed before Sándor's eyes. Sándor, however, played the "Blue Danube" waltz, and received an extra ration of food for his performance.

as at hundreds of other camps in the Reich and occupied Europe where the Germans used slave laborers, prisoners were also employed outside the camps, in coal mines and rock quarries, and on construction projects, digging tunnels and canals. Under armed guard, they shoveled snow off roads and cleared rubble from roads and towns hit during air raids. A large number of slave laborers eventually were used in factories that produced weapons and other goods that supported the German war effort. Many private companies, such as I. G. Farben and Bavarian Motor Works (BMW), which produced automobile and airplane engines, eagerly sought the use of prisoners as a source of cheap labor.

Escape from Auschwitz-Birkenau was almost impossible. Electrically charged barbed-wire fences surrounded both the concentration camp and the killing center. Guards, equipped with machine guns and automatic rifles, stood in the many watchtowers. The lives of the prisoners were completely controlled by their guards, who on a whim could inflict cruel punishments on them. Prisoners were also mistreated by fellow inmates who were chosen to supervise the others in return for special favors by the guards.

Cruel "medical experiments" were conducted at Auschwitz-Birkenau. Men, women, and children were used as subjects. SS physician Dr. Josef Mengele carried out painful and traumatic experiments on dwarfs and twins, including young children. The aim of some experiments was to find better medical treatments for German soldiers and airmen. Other experiments were aimed at improving methods of sterilizing people the Nazis considered inferior. Many people died during the experiments. Others were killed after the "research" was completed and their organs removed for further study.

Most prisoners at Auschwitz-Birkenau survived only a few weeks or months. Those who were too ill or too weak to work were condemned to death in the gas chambers. Some committed suicide by throwing themselves against the electric wires. Others resembled walking corpses, broken in body and spirit. Yet other inmates were determined to stay alive.

Inset: Women at forced labor in the Ravensbrück concentration camp. Ravensbrück, Germany, wartime. *Suddeutscher Verlag Bilderdienst, Munich, Germany.*

Inmates at forced labor in the Mauthausen concentration camp. Mauthausen, Austria, 1942, *National Archives, Washington,* D.C.

Prisoners working in the BMW aircraft factory. Allach, Germany, wartime. *Bayerische Motorenwerke AG, Historisches Archiv, Munich, Germany.*

Prisoners of the Camps

As the Jews were the main targets of Nazi genocide, the victims of the killing centers were overwhelmingly Jewish. In the hundreds of slave labor and concentration camps not equipped with gassing facilities, however, other individuals from a broad range of backgrounds could also be found. Prisoners were required to wear color-coded triangles on their jackets so that the guards and officers of the camps could easily identify each person's background and pit the different groups against each other. Political prisoners, such as Communists, Socialists, and trade unionists wore red triangles. Common criminals wore green. Gypsies and others the Germans considered "anti-social" or "shiftless" wore black triangles. Jehovah's Witnesses wore purple and homosexuals pink. Letters indicated nationality: for example, P stood for Polish, SU for Soviet Union, F for French.

Captured Soviet soldiers worked as slave laborers, and many of these prisoners of war died because they were executed or badly mistreated by the Germans. In all, over three million died at the hands of the Germans.

Twenty-three thousand German and Austrian Gypsies were inmates of Auschwitz-Birkenau, and about 20,000 of these were killed there. Men, women, and children were confined together in a separate Gypsy family camp. On the night of August 2, 1944, a large group of Gypsies was gassed in the destruction of the Gypsy family camp. Nearly 3,000 Gypsies were murdered, including most of the women and children. Some of the men were sent to slave labor camps in Germany, where many died. Altogether, hundreds of thousands of Gypsies from all over German-occupied Europe were murdered in camps and by mobile killing squads.

Political prisoners, Jehovah's Witnesses, and homosexuals were sent to concentration camps as punishment. Members of these three groups were not targeted, as were Jews and Gypsies, for systematic murder. Nevertheless, many died in the camps from starvation, disease, exhaustion, and brutal treatment.

Grini Bredtveit
Berg

Vaivara
Lagedi
Klooga
Kaiserwald

N

Horseroed

Front Line
January 1944

Bergen-Belsen   Neuengamme   Stutthof   Koldichevo   Treblinka
Westerbork   Skarzysko-Kamienna
Vught   Ravensbrueck   Majdanek
Breendonck   Sachsenhausen   Sobibor
Mechelen   Dora-Mittelbau   Chelmno   Trawniki   Budzyn
Niederhagen   Belzec
Wevelsburg   Gross Rosen   Janowska   Poniatowa
Compiegne   Buchenwald   Belzec
Drancy   Fuenfbrunnen   Flossenbuerg   Starachowice
ATLANTIC   Mauthausen
OCEAN   Vittel   Strasshof   Plaszow
Schirmeck-   Dachau Gunskirchen   Auschwitz
Vorbruck   Kistarcsa
Natzweiler-   Bolzano   La Risiera
Struthof   de San Sabba
Gurs   Sajmiste
Rivesaltes   Topovske Supe
Fossoli di Carpi   Sabac   Nis

Baron de Hirsch

Front Line
January 1944

Solid squares represent a
sampling of camps. Because
of map scale, not all camps
can be shown or labeled. Camps
operated by German-allied or
dependent states are not shown.

EUROPE
MAJOR NAZI CAMPS

0   400
MILES

German Reich &
Occupied Territories
German Allies or
Dependent States
Neutrals   Allies
⊡ Extermination Camps
▪ Other Camps

Polish children imprisoned in Auschwitz before their deportation to Germany. Some 50,000 Polish children were kidnapped from their parents for adoption by German parents. Auschwitz, Poland, July 1944. *Central State Archive of the October Revolution, Byelorussia.*

Willibald Wohlfahrt was 14 when he saw his oldest brother being taken away to a concentration camp because he was a Jehovah's Witness, and his brother Gregor executed for refusing to join the German military. In 1941 Willibald and his remaining brothers and sisters were taken away by the Nazis. Willibald was sent to a Catholic convent, where a Nazi instructor tried to turn him into a loyal follower of the Reich. When Allied armies approached Germany, Willibald was sent to the battle front to dig trenches for the German home defense. He was killed in 1945 while digging trenches in western Germany. He was 17 years old.

In 1944, when Joseph Müller was12, he was taken from his classroom by two strangers who said he had "appendicitis" and needed immediate surgery. He protested, but was beaten and forcefully taken into surgery where, like other Gypsies, he was sterilized. After his recovery, Joseph was to be deported to the Bergen-Belsen concentration camp in northwestern Germany. But Joseph was luckier than many Gypsies, as his foster father managed to have him smuggled from the hospital and hidden. Joseph survived the remainder of the war by hiding for five months in a garden shed.

Harry Pauly was 29 when he was turned in by two boys pressured by the Gestapo to denounce homosexuals, and was again sentenced in 1943. He was again released after some friends in the theater intervened on his behalf. He was drafted into the army but was perpetually harassed by people who knew of his homosexuality. He deserted twice, was caught, and was sent to a special penal combat unit in which almost everyone was killed. Somehow he managed to survive.

The Polish Catholic Julian Noga was 20 when he was arrested in 1941 for continuing to see his German girlfriend. He was imprisoned and then transferred to the Flossenbürg concentration camp near the Czechoslovakian border to do backbreaking work in a quarry.

Gypsy children imprisoned in Bełżec labor camp. Bełżec, Poland, c. 1940. *Archives of Mechanical Documentation, Warsaw, Poland.*

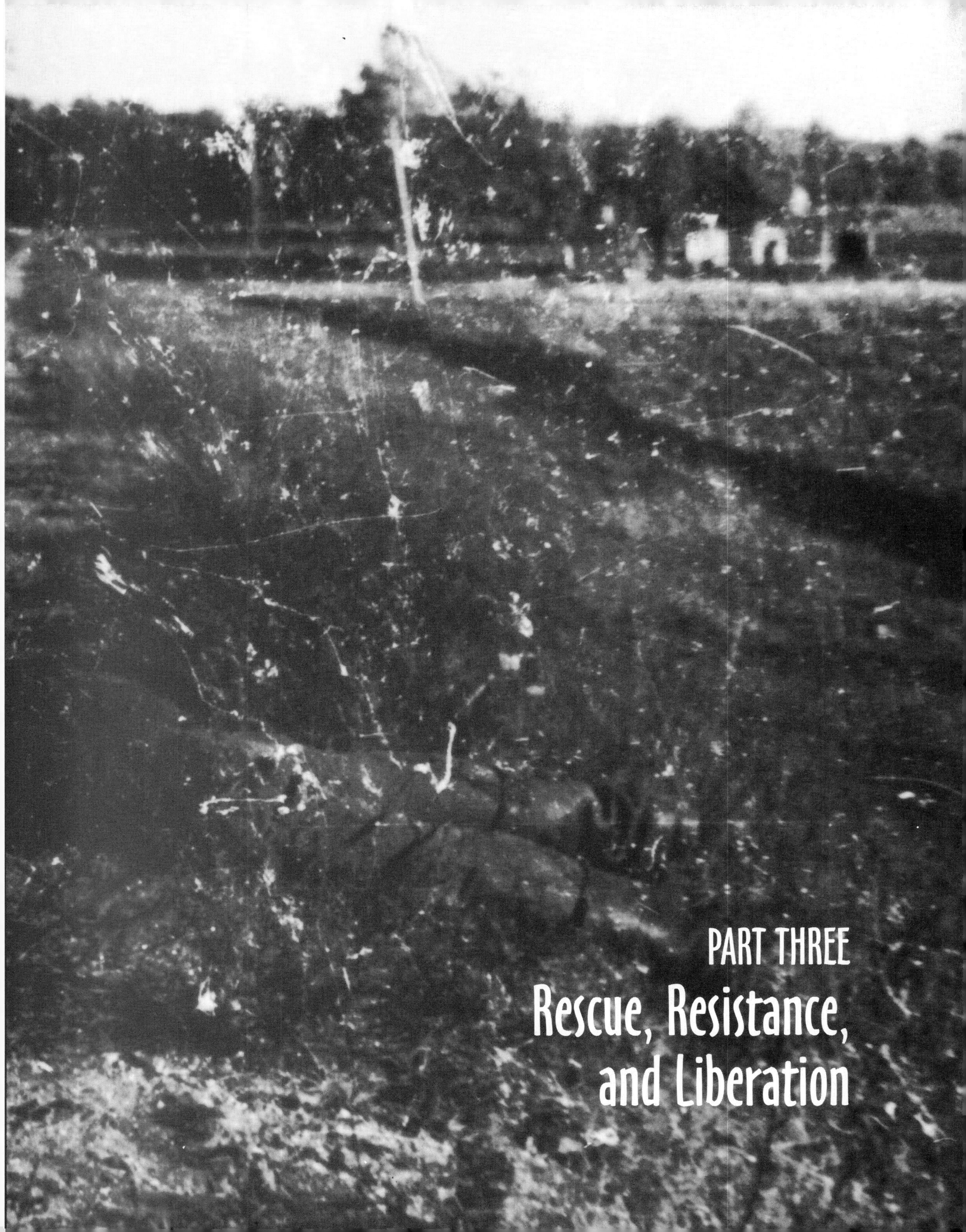

PART THREE
Rescue, Resistance, and Liberation

Rescue

Preben Munch-Nielsen, a Protestant, grew up in the small Danish fishing village of Snekkersten, 25 miles north of Copenhagen. After the Germans occupied Denmark in 1940, 14-year-old Preben joined the resistance as a courier. Preben became involved in the national rescue effort. He helped transport 1,400 Jewish refugees to Sweden.

In 1940, when she was 10, Irene Freund was deported with her parents from Germany to Gurs and then Rivesaltes, internment camps in southern France. A Jewish children's aid society took Irene out of the camp and brought her to a Catholic convent along with 13 other Jewish girls. She would never again see her parents, who were deported on August 14, 1942, to Auschwitz-Birkenau, where they perished.

Previous page: Partisan Boris Yochai planting dynamite on a railroad track near Vilna. He blew up twelve trains. Vilna, Lithuania, USSR, 1943–1944. YIVO Institute for Jewish Research, New York, N.Y.

Most individuals in occupied Europe did not actively collaborate in the Nazi genocide. Nor did they do anything to help Jews and other victims of Nazi policies. Throughout the Holocaust, millions of people silently stood by while they saw Jews, Gypsies, and other "enemies of the Reich" being rounded up and deported. Many of these bystanders told themselves that what they saw happening was none of their business. Others were too frightened to help. In many places, providing shelter to Jews was a crime punishable by death.

In spite of the risks, a small number of individuals refused to stand by and watch. These people had the courage to help by providing hiding places, underground escape routes, false papers, food, clothing, money, and sometimes even weapons.

Denmark was the only occupied country that actively resisted the Nazi regime's attempts to deport its Jewish citizens. On September 28, 1943, Georg Ferdinand Duckwitz, a German diplomat, secretly informed the Danish resistance that the Nazis were planning to deport the Danish Jews. The Danes responded quickly, organizing a nationwide effort to smuggle the Jews by sea to neutral Sweden. Warned of the German plans, Jews began to leave Copenhagen, where most of the 8,000 Jews in Denmark lived, and other cities, by train, car, and on foot. With the help of the Danish people, they found hiding places in homes, hospitals, and churches. Within a two-week period fishermen helped ferry 7,220 Danish Jews and 680 non-Jewish family members to safety across the narrow body of water separating Denmark from Sweden.

The Danish rescue effort was unique because it was nationwide. It was not completely successful, however. Almost 500 Danish Jews were deported to the Theresienstadt ghetto in Czechoslovakia. Yet even of these Jews, all but 51 survived the Holocaust, largely because the Danish Red Cross sent food to the Jews in the ghetto, and because Danish officials pressured the Germans with their concerns for the well-being of those who had been deported. The Danes proved that widespread support for Jews and resistance to Nazi policies could save lives.

There are numerous stories of brave people in other countries who also tried to save the Jews from perishing at the hands of the Nazis. Nearly 12,000 Jewish children were rescued by clergymen in France who found housing for them and even smuggled some into Switzerland and Spain. About 20,000 Polish Jews were able to survive in hiding outside the ghetto in Warsaw because people provided shelter for them in their homes. Some Jews were even hidden in the Warsaw Zoo by the zoo's director, Jan Zabinski.

Danish citizens fleeing from German-occupied Denmark to neutral Sweden. This group probably includes members of the Danish resistance. Denmark, c. summer 1944. *Museum for Denmark's Fight for Freedom, 1941–1945, Copenhagen, Denmark.*

The War Refugee Board

It was not until late in the war that the United States attempted to rescue Jews from the Holocaust. In January 1944, the Secretary of the Treasury, Henry Morgenthau, Jr., persuaded President Franklin D. Roosevelt to establish the War Refugee Board.

Although confirmed reports of the mass murders of Jews had reached the U.S. State Department in 1942, officials had remained silent. During the war the State Department had insisted that the best way to save victims of Nazi Germany's policies was to win the war as quickly as possible.

The War Refugee Board worked with Jewish organizations, diplomats from neutral countries, and resistance groups in Europe to rescue Jews from occupied territories and provide relief to inmates of Nazi concentration camps. Its most extensive rescue efforts were led by Raoul Wallenberg, a Swedish diplomat based in Budapest, Hungary. Wallenberg helped protect tens of thousands of Hungarian Jews from being deported to Auschwitz by distributing protective Swedish passports. Because Sweden was a neutral country, Germany could not easily harm Swedish citizens. Wallenberg also set up hospitals, nurseries, and soup kitchens for the Jews of Budapest.*

The War Refugee Board played a crucial role in the rescue of as many as 200,000 Jews. However, some people still wonder how many more Jews might have been saved if the rescue missions had begun sooner.

---

* Wallenberg disappeared during the Soviet liberation of Budapest. He was seen for the last time in the company of Soviet troops on January 17, 1945. Ten years later, the Soviet Union admitted that he had been arrested and claimed that he died in prison in 1947.

Swedish diplomat Raoul
Wallenberg in his office in
Budapest. Budapest, Hungary.
November 26, 1944. *Photo:*
Thomas Veres, New York, N.Y.

Resistance Inside Germany

Despite the high risk of being caught by police with the help of their many informers, some individuals and groups attempted to resist Nazism even in Germany. Socialists, Communists, trade unionists, and others clandestinely wrote, printed, and distributed anti-Nazi literature. Many of these rebels were arrested and imprisoned in concentration camps.

There were many plots to assassinate Hitler during the war. After the important Soviet victory at Stalingrad in early 1943, when it looked as though the tide was turning against the German army, a serious assassination attempt was planned by a group of German military officers and carried out in 1944. Hitler escaped the bomb blast with minor injuries. The four leaders of the conspiracy were immediately shot. Later, two hundred other individuals convicted of involvement in the plot were executed.

Of the Germans who opposed Hitler's dictatorship, only one group openly protested the Nazi genocide against Jews. The "White Rose" movement was founded in June 1942 by Hans Scholl, a 24-year-old medical student at the University of Munich, his 22-year-old sister Sophie, and 24-year-old Christoph Probst. Although the exact origin of the name "White Rose" is unknown, it clearly stands for purity and innocence in the face of evil. Hans, Sophie, and Christoph were outraged that educated Germans went along with Nazi policies. They distributed anti-Nazi leaflets and painted slogans like "Freedom!" and "Down with Hitler!" on walls of the university. In February 1943, Hans and Sophie Scholl were caught distributing leaflets and arrested. Together with their friend Christoph, they were executed four days later. Hans's last words were "Long live freedom!"

Hans Scholl, Sophie Scholl,
and Christoph Probst, leaders
of the "White Rose" resistance
group. Germany, summer
1942. *Dr. George Wittenstein,
Santa Barbara, California.*

The Warsaw Ghetto Uprising

Many Jews in ghettos across eastern Europe tried to organize resistance against the Germans and to arm themselves with smuggled and homemade weapons. Between 1941 and 1943 underground resistance movements formed in about 100 Jewish ghettos. The most famous attempt by Jews to resist the Germans in armed fighting occurred in the Warsaw ghetto.

In the summer of 1942, about 300,000 Jews were deported from Warsaw to Treblinka. When reports of mass murder in the killing center leaked back to the Warsaw ghetto, a surviving group of mostly young people formed an organization called the Z.O.B. (for the Polish name, *Zydowska Organizacja Bojowa*, which means Jewish Fighting Organization). The Z.O.B., led by 23-year-old Mordecai Anielewicz, issued a proclamation calling for the Jewish people to resist going to the railroad cars. In January 1943, Warsaw ghetto fighters fired upon German troops as they tried to round up another group of ghetto inhabitants for deportation. Fighters used a small supply of weapons that had been smuggled into the ghetto. After a few days, the troops retreated. This small victory inspired the ghetto fighters to prepare for future resistance.

On April 19, 1943, the Warsaw ghetto uprising began after German troops and police entered the ghetto to deport its surviving inhabitants. Seven hundred and fifty fighters fought the heavily armed and well-trained Germans. The ghetto fighters were able to hold out for nearly a month, but on May 16, 1943, the revolt ended. The Germans had slowly crushed the resistance. Of the more than 56,000 Jews captured, about 7,000 were shot, and the remainder were deported to killing centers or concentration camps.

Roundup of Jews during the
Warsaw ghetto uprising.
Warsaw, Poland, April 19–May
16, 1943. *National Archives,
Washington*, D.C.

Killing Center Revolts

Joseph Gani was selected for slave labor after he arrived at Auschwitz-Birkenau in 1944. On October 7 of that year he joined in the uprising started by the Sonderkommando. *Sometime after the uprising, Joseph was killed in Birkenau.*

The Warsaw ghetto uprising inspired revolts in other ghettos and in killing centers. Although many resisters knew they were bound to lose against overwhelmingly superior German forces, they chose to die fighting.

After the last Jews deported to Treblinka were gassed in May 1943, about 1,000 Jewish prisoners remained in the camp. Aware that they were soon to be killed, the prisoners decided to revolt. On August 2, armed with shovels, picks, and a few weapons stolen from the arms warehouse, they set fire to part of the camp and broke through its barbed-wire fence. About 200 prisoners managed to escape, and about half of them survived German efforts to recapture them.

Two inmates of Sobibór, Aleksandr Pechersky and Leon Feldhendler, planned a similar revolt in 1943. On October 14, prisoners killed eleven camp guards and set the camp on fire. About 300 prisoners escaped, but many were killed during the manhunt that followed. Fifty were alive at the war's end.

At Auschwitz-Birkenau, prisoners of the *Sonderkommando* — the special squad whose job it was to burn the corpses of the murdered victims — learned of the plans to kill them. On October 7, 1944, a group of them rebelled, killing three guards and blowing up the crematorium. Several hundred prisoners escaped, but most were later recaptured and killed. Four young women accused of supplying the dynamite were hanged in front of the remaining inmates. One of them, 23-year-old Roza Robota, shouted, "Be strong, have courage" as the trap door opened.

Crematorium at Auschwitz-Birkenau, Poland, 1942-1943. Corpses were burned in ovens housed inside the brick building. This crematorium would be dynamited by rebelling inmates on October 7, 1944. *Main Commission for the Investigation of Nazi War Crimes in Poland, Warsaw, Poland.*

Roza Robota, Jewish underground resistance member who helped supply dynamite used to blow up the crematorium. *Yad Vashem, Jerusalem, Israel.*

Jewish Partisans

Because Gad Beck was the child of a mixed marriage (only one parent was Jewish), he was spared deportation to the east. He remained in Berlin, where he became active in the underground, helping Jews to escape to Switzerland. A homosexual, he was able to turn to his trusted non-Jewish homosexual acquaintances to help supply food and hiding places. In early 1945 a Jewish spy for the Gestapo betrayed Gad and a number of his underground friends. He was interned in a transit camp in Berlin.

Some Jews who managed to escape from ghettos and camps formed their own fighting units. These fighters, or partisans, were concentrated in densely wooded areas. A large group of partisans in occupied Soviet territory hid in a forest near the Lithuanian capital of Vilna. They were able to derail hundreds of trains and kill over 3,000 German soldiers.

Life as a partisan in the forests was difficult. People had to move from place to place to avoid discovery, raid farmers' food supplies to eat, and try to survive the winter in flimsy shelters built from logs and branches. In some places, partisans received assistance from local villagers, but more often they could not count on help, partly because of widespread antisemitism, partly because of people's fears of being severely punished for helping. The partisans lived in constant danger of local informers revealing their whereabouts to the Germans.

Many Jews participated in the partisan units formed in France and Italy to help regular Allied forces defeat German forces. They forged documents and identity cards, printed anti-Nazi leaflets, and assassinated collaborators.

Twenty-three-year-old Hannah Senesh, a Hungarian Jew who emigrated to Palestine in 1939, was one of the thirty-two Palestinian parachutists the British dropped behind German lines to organize resistance and rescue efforts. Before crossing the border into Hungary on June 7, 1944, to warn Hungarian Jews about the extermination camps, Senesh, a poet, handed a poem to one of her companions. It ended with these lines:

> *Blessed is the heart with strength to stop its beating*
> *for honor's sake*
> *Blessed is the match consumed in kindling flame.*

Senesh was captured the next day and executed as a traitor to Hungary.

Members of a "family" camp set up by partisan Tuvia Bielsky in the Naliboki forest in Poland. Most partisan groups were made up of able-bodied, single men, armed for combat. Bielsky's special camp was created after he and other family members escaped from the mobile killing units shooting tens of thousands of Jews in western Byelorussia. *Yad Vashem, Jerusalem, Israel.*

Hannah Senesh and her brother Giora in Palestine a few months before she left for her mission in Europe. Haifa, Palestine, December 1944. *Beit Hannah Senesh, Kibbutz Sdot Yam, Israel.*

Death Marches

When he was 24, Majlech Kisielnicki was put on a forced march out of Auschwitz-Birkenau on January 18, 1945, and later continued the ordeal by train. In the middle of one night, the train stopped, unable to continue because the rail lines had been bombed. Majlech and the other inmates were taken off the train and marched into Germany. After a few days walking in the freezing cold, they came to a town called Waldenbürg, where there were mines dug into the mountainside. The Germans locked Majlech and the others in the mine overnight. When they came to open the gates in the morning, they found the corpses of many men who had suffocated.

Near the end of the war, when Germany's military force was collapsing, the Allied armies closed in on the Nazi concentration camps. The Soviets approached from the east, and the British, French, and Americans from the west. The Germans began frantically to move the prisoners out of the camps near the front and take them to be used as slave laborers in camps inside Germany. Prisoners were first taken by train and then by foot on "death marches," as they became known. Prisoners were forced to march long distances in bitter cold, with little or no food, water, or rest. Those who could not keep up were shot.

The largest death marches took place in the winter of 1944–1945, when the Soviet army began its liberation of Poland. Just hours before the Soviets arrived at Auschwitz, the Germans marched 60,000 prisoners out of the camp toward Wodzislaw, a town thirty-five miles away, where they were put on freight trains to other camps. About one in four died on the way.

The Nazis often killed large groups of prisoners before, during, or after marches. During one march, seven thousand Jewish prisoners, six thousand of them women, were moved from camps in the Danzig region bordered on the north by the Baltic Sea. On the ten-day march, seven hundred were murdered. Those still alive when the marchers reached the shores of the sea were driven into the water and shot.

Prisoners from Dachau during
a death march. Grunewald,
Germany, April 29, 1945. *KZ-
Gedenkstätte Dachau Ost, Munich,
Germany*.

Liberation

Soviet soldiers were the first to liberate concentration camp prisoners in the final stages of the war. On July 23, 1944, they entered the Majdanek concentration camp in Poland, and later overran several other killing centers. On January 27, 1945, they entered Auschwitz-Birkenau and there found hundreds of sick and exhausted prisoners. The Germans had been forced to leave these prisoners behind in their hasty retreat from the camp. Also left behind were victims' belongings: 348,820 men's suits, 836,255 women's coats, and tens of thousands of pairs of shoes.

British, Canadian, American, and French troops also freed prisoners from the camps. The Americans were responsible for liberating Buchenwald and Dachau, while British forces entered Bergen-Belsen. Although the Germans had attempted to empty the camps of surviving prisoners and hide all evidence of their crimes, the Allied soldiers came upon thousands of dead bodies "stacked up like cordwood," according to one American soldier. The prisoners who were still alive were living skeletons.

Bill Barrett, an American army journalist, described what he saw at Dachau: "There were about a dozen bodies in the dirty boxcar, men and women alike. They had gone without

Survivor of the Buchenwald concentration camp after liberation. Buchenwald, Germany, 1945. *National Archives, Washington, D.C.*

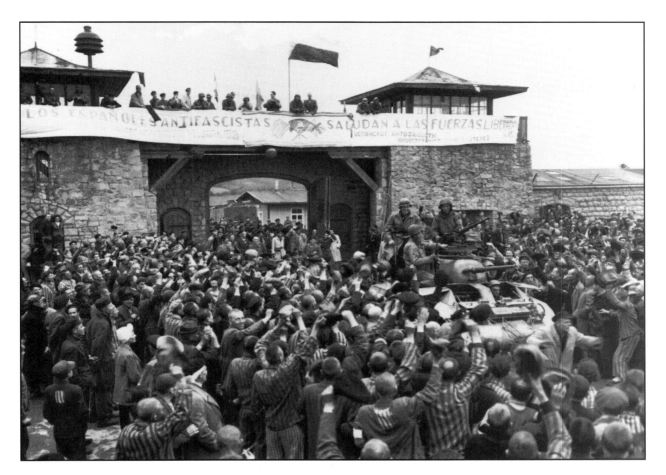

food so long that their dead wrists were broomsticks tipped with claws. These were the victims of a deliberate starvation diet. . . ."

Allied troops, physicians, and relief workers tried to provide nourishment for the surviving prisoners, but many of them were too weak to digest the food and could not be saved. In spite of the liberators' efforts, many camp survivors died. Half of the prisoners discovered alive in Auschwitz died within a few days of being freed.

Survivors had mixed reactions to their newfound freedom. While a few looked forward to being reunited with other family members, some felt guilty for surviving when so many of their relatives and friends had died. Some felt overwhelmed, as one survivor, Viktor Frankl, a psychiatrist, expressed: "Timidly, we looked around and glanced at each other questioningly. Then we ventured a few steps out of the camp. This time no orders were shouted at us, nor was there any need to duck quickly to avoid a blow or a kick. 'Freedom,' we repeated to ourselves, and yet we could not grasp it."

Mauthausen concentration camp survivors cheer U.S. soldiers two days after liberation. Mauthausen, Austria, May 9, 1945. *National Archives, Washington, D.C.*

The Nuremberg Trials

After the war, some of those responsible for the crimes of the Holocaust were brought to trial. Nuremberg, Germany, was chosen as a site for trials that took place in 1945 and 1946. Judges from the Allied Powers — Great Britain, France, the Soviet Union, and the United States — presided over the hearings of twenty-two major Nazi criminals. Twelve prominent Nazis were sentenced to death. Most of the defendants admitted the crimes of which they were accused, although most claimed that they were simply following the orders of a higher authority. Those individuals directly involved in the killing received the most severe sentences. Other people who played key roles in the Holocaust, including high-level government officials, and business executives who used concentration camp inmates as slave laborers, received short prison sentences or no penalty at all.

The Nazis' highest authority, the person most to blame for the Holocaust, was missing at the trials. Adolf Hitler had committed suicide in the final days of the war, as did several of his closest aides. Many more criminals were never tried. Some fled Germany to live abroad, including hundreds who came to the United States.

Trials of Nazis continued to take place both in Germany and many other countries. Simon Wiesenthal, a Nazi-hunter, located Adolf Eichmann in Argentina. Eichmann, who had helped plan and carry out the deportations of millions of Jews, was brought to trial in Israel. The testimony of hundreds of witnesses, many of them survivors, was followed all over the world. Eichmann was found guilty and executed in 1962.

Nuremberg trial of Nazi war
criminals. Nuremberg,
Germany, 1946. *National
Archives, Washington*, D.C.

The Survivors

For the survivors, returning to life as it had been before the Holocaust was impossible. Jewish communities no longer existed in much of Europe. When people tried to return to their homes from camps or hiding places, they found that, in many cases, their homes had been looted or taken over by others.

Returning home was also dangerous. After the war, anti-Jewish riots broke out in several Polish cities. The largest anti-Jewish pogrom took place in July 1946 in Kielce, a city in southeastern Poland. When 150 Jews returned to the city, people living there feared that hundreds more would come back to reclaim their houses and belongings. Age-old antisemitic myths, such as Jews' ritual murders of Christians, arose once again. After a rumor spread that Jews had killed a Polish boy to use his blood in religious rituals, a mob attacked the group of survivors. The rioters killed 41 people and wounded 50 more. News of the Kielce pogrom spread rapidly, and Jews realized that there was no future for them in Poland.

Many survivors ended up in displaced person (DP) camps set up in western Europe under Allied military occupation at the sites of former concentration camps. There they waited to be admitted to places like the United States, South Africa, or Palestine. At first, many countries continued their old immigration policies, which greatly limited the number of refugees they would accept. The British government, which controlled Palestine, refused to let large numbers of Jews in. Many Jews tried to enter Palestine without legal papers, and when caught some were held in camps on the island of Cyprus, while others were deported back to Germany. Great Britain's scandalous treatment of Jewish refugees added to international pressures for a homeland for the Jewish people. Finally, the United Nations voted to divide Palestine into a Jewish and an Arab state. Early in 1948, the British began withdrawing from Palestine. On May 14, 1948, one of the leading voices for a Jewish homeland, David Ben-Gurion, announced the formation of the State of Israel. After this, Jewish refugee ships freely landed in the seaports of the new

Concentration camp survivors arriving in New York at a hospitality center staffed by United Service for New Americans and financed by the United Jewish Appeal, a major Jewish charitable organization. New York, 1946–1952. *Hebrew Immigrant Aid Society, New York, N. Y.*

nation. The United States also changed its immigration policy to allow more Jewish refugees to enter.

Although many Jewish survivors were able to build new lives in their adopted countries, many non-Jewish victims of Nazi policies continued to be persecuted in Germany. Laws which discriminated against Roma (Gypsies) continued to be in effect until 1970 in some parts of the country. The law used in Nazi Germany to imprison homosexuals remained in effect until 1969.

Below are some of the survivors who were able to give testimony about what they experienced during the Holocaust. They told their stories to their children and grandchildren as a tribute to the loved ones who did not survive.

 In July 1944, Irene Freund was freed in France by Allied troops. After being transferred to several children's homes in France, she emigrated to the United States in 1947.

 On April 29, 1945, Sándor Braun was liberated in Dachau by American troops. In 1950 he emigrated to the United States, where he became a composer and a professional violinist and was known as Shony Alex Braun.

 On April 23, 1945, Julian Noga was liberated while on a forced march from the Flossenbürg concentration camp. He was reunited with his girlfriend, Frieda, after the war, and they emigrated to the United States.

 After the war, Majlech Kisielnicki returned to his hometown, Kałuszyn, Poland, where he was reunited with his older brother Abram. They both emigrated to the United States and eventually ran an import-export business in New York. Majlech married, and he and his wife started a family.

On May 1, 1945, Judith Kàlmàn was liberated at Seehausen, a subcamp of Dachau. She weighed 48 pounds. Judith eventually married and moved to France. In 1948 the couple emigrated to the United States, started a small business, and raised three daughters.

Teenage orphans, survivors of Buchenwald, leaving for Switzerland. There a United Nations relief group will help them find new homes. Buchenwald, Germany, April, 1945. *Franklin D. Roosevelt Library, Hyde Park, N.Y.*

Barbara Ledermann remained in hiding in Holland until April 1945, when Amsterdam was liberated by Canadian troops. She emigrated to the United States in 1947.

After the war, Gad Beck helped organize the emigration of Jewish survivors to Palestine. In 1947 he left for Palestine, and returned to Berlin in 1979.

After the war, Harry Pauly started his own small theater in Germany.

In April 1945, Wolfgang Munzer was liberated by Soviet soldiers while on a forced march from the Oranienburg concentration camp near Berlin. He emigrated to the United States in 1947 and settled in the Boston area with his wife, also a Holocaust survivor.

On April 15, 1945, Margot Heumann was liberated by the British at Bergen-Belsen. She was taken by the Swedish Red Cross to Stockholm, where she lived for more than a year with a Swedish schoolteacher before emigrating to the United States. She settled in New York, continued her schooling, and worked in an advertising agency. She married and had two children.

After liberation, Helga Leeser, her sister, and her mother remained in Rotterdam, where they had hidden during the war.

Afterword: Remembering the Children

Anne Frank was just four in 1933, when her parents decided to flee their home in Nazi Germany for the safety of Amsterdam, the capital of the Netherlands. In 1942, when she was thirteen, she and her family were forced into hiding in a small attic. While there Anne recorded her observations in a diary. In 1944, she and her family were discovered by the Nazis. Anne and her older sister, Margot, were sent to Westerbork transit camp, to Auschwitz-Birkenau, and then to the Bergen-Belsen camp, where they both perished. Anne's father, Otto, survived and arranged to have Anne's diary published as a testimony about the Holocaust.

Because of her now-famous diary, Anne Frank may be the most well-known child victim of the Holocaust. As we have seen, more than one million other children, ranging in age from infants to older teenagers, were persecuted and murdered by the Nazi government and its collaborators between 1933 and 1945. At the United States Holocaust Memorial Museum in Washington, D.C., the Wall of Remembrance stands as a special memorial to these children. The Wall displays over 3,000 ceramic tiles created by elementary and middle-school students from across the United States. After learning about the history of the Holocaust, these students, who come from diverse racial and religious backgrounds, created the tiles as a way of expressing their thoughts and feelings about the Holocaust and its victims. "I thought it should be forgotten but my friends opened my eyes," wrote Terri Arendt. "Hope lives when people remember" were another student's words. Still another tile, showing a forearm with the tattooed number of a concentration camp, is captioned: "You can't erase memories." One tile's words, "Tell Israel and Sarah We Remember," inspired the title of this book.

After confronting the horrors of the Holocaust, many young people, as well as adults, have more questions than answers. The most pressing question of all stands in bold letters on one of the tiles: "Why?" May we not be afraid to ask ourselves these difficult questions as we try to understand how the Holocaust could have happened.

Anne Frank at her writing desk,
before she went into hiding.
Amsterdam, Netherlands,
1940. *Anne Frank Foundation,*
Amsterdam, Netherlands.

CHRONOLOGY

January 30, 1933	Adolf Hitler is appointed Chancellor of Germany.
February 28, 1933	German government takes away freedom of speech, assembly, press, and freedom from invasion of privacy (mail, telephone, telegraph) and from house search without warrant.
March 4, 1933	Franklin D. Roosevelt is inaugurated President of the United States.
March 20, 1933	First concentration camp opens at Dachau, Germany, for political opponents of the regime.
April 1, 1933	Nationwide boycott of Jewish-owned businesses in Germany is carried out under Nazi leadership.
April 7, 1933	Law excludes "non-Aryans" from government employment; Jewish civil servants, including university professors and schoolteachers, are fired in Germany.
May 10, 1933	Books written by Jews, political opponents of Nazis, and many others are burned during huge public rallies across Germany.
July 14, 1933	Law passed in Germany permitting the forced sterilization of Gypsies, the mentally and physically disabled, African-Germans, and others considered "inferior" or "unfit."
October 1934	First major wave of arrests of homosexuals occurs throughout Germany, continuing into November.
April 1935	Jehovah's Witnesses are banned from all civil service jobs and are arrested throughout Germany.
September 15, 1935	Citizenship and racial laws are announced at Nazi party rally in Nuremberg.

March 7, 1936	Hitler's army invades the Rhineland.
July 12, 1936	First German Gypsies are arrested and deported to Dachau concentration camp.
Summer 1936	Olympic Games take place in Berlin. Anti-Jewish signs are removed until the Games are over.
March 13, 1938	Austria is annexed by Germany.
July 6–15, 1938	Representatives from thirty-two countries meet at Evian, France, to discuss refugee policies. Most of the countries refuse to let in more Jewish refugees.
November 9–10, 1938	Nazis burn synagogues and loot Jewish homes and businesses in nationwide pogroms called "Kristallnacht" ("Night of Broken Glass"). Nearly 30,000 German and Austrian Jewish men are deported to concentration camps. Many Jewish women are jailed.
November 15, 1938	All Jewish children are expelled from public schools. Segregated Jewish schools are created.
December 2–3, 1938	All Gypsies in the Reich are required to register with the police.
March 15, 1939	German troops invade Czechoslovakia.
June 1939	Cuba and the United States refuse to accept Jewish refugees aboard the ship S.S. *St. Louis*, which is forced to return to Europe.
September 1, 1939	Germany invades Poland; World War II begins.

October 1939	Hitler extends power of doctors to kill institutionalized mentally and physically disabled persons in the "euthanasia" program.
Spring 1940	Germany invades and defeats Denmark, Norway, Belgium, Luxembourg, Holland, and France.
October 1940	Warsaw ghetto is established.
March 22, 1941	Gypsy and African-German children are expelled from public schools in the Reich.
March 24, 1941	Germany invades North Africa.
April 6, 1941	Germany invades Yugoslavia and Greece.
June 22, 1941	German army invades the Soviet Union. The *Einsatzgruppen*, mobile killing squads, begin mass murders of Jews, Gypsies, and Communist leaders.
September 23, 1941	Soviet prisoners of war and Polish prisoners are killed in Nazi tests of gas chambers at Auschwitz in occupied Poland.
September 28–29, 1941	Nearly 34,000 Jews are murdered by mobile killing squads at Babi Yar, near Kiev (Ukraine).
October–November 1941	First group of German and Austrian Jews are deported to ghettos in eastern Europe.
December 7, 1941	Japan attacks Pearl Harbor.
December 8, 1941	Gassing operations begin at Chełmno "extermination" camp in occupied Poland.

December 11, 1941	Germany declares war on the United States.
January 20, 1942	Fifteen Nazi and government leaders meet at Wannsee, a section of Berlin, to discuss the "final solution to the Jewish question."
1942	Nazi "extermination" camps located in occupied Poland at Auschwitz-Birkenau, Treblinka, Sobibór, Bełżec, and Majdanek-Lublin begin mass murder of Jews in gas chambers.
June 1, 1942	Jews in France and Holland are required to wear identifying stars.
April 19–May 16, 1943	Jews in the Warsaw ghetto resist with arms the Germans' attempt to deport them to the Nazi extermination camps.
August 2, 1943	Inmates revolt at Treblinka.
Fall 1943	Danes use boats to smuggle most of the nation's Jews to neutral Sweden.
October 14, 1943	Inmates at Sobibór begin armed revolt.
January 1944	President Roosevelt sets up the War Refugee Board at the urging of Treasury Secretary Henry Morgenthau, Jr.
March 19, 1944	Germany occupies Hungary.
May 15–July 9, 1944	Over 430,000 Hungarian Jews are deported to Auschwitz-Birkenau, where most of them are gassed.
June 6, 1944	Allied powers invade western Europe on D-Day.

July 20, 1944	German officers fail in their attempt to assassinate Hitler.
July 23, 1944	Soviet troops arrive at Majdanek concentration camp.
August 2, 1944	Nazis destroy the Gypsy camp at Auschwitz-Birkenau; around 3,000 Gypsies are gassed.
October 7, 1944	Prisoners at Auschwitz-Birkenau revolt and blow up one crematorium.
January 17, 1945	Nazis evacuate Auschwitz; prisoners begin "death marches" toward Germany.
January 27, 1945	Soviet troops enter Auschwitz.
April 1945	U.S. troops liberate survivors at Buchenwald and Dachau concentration camps.
April 30, 1945	Hitler commits suicide in his bunker in Berlin.
May 5, 1945	U.S. troops liberate Mauthausen concentration camp.
May 7, 1945	Germany surrenders and the war ends in Europe.
November 1945 – October 1946	War crime trials held at Nuremberg, Germany.
May 14, 1948	State of Israel is established.

Survivors of Buchenwald
concentration camp.
Buchenwald, Germany, 1945.
Margaret Bourke-White,
Time-Life Photo, New York, N.Y.

Suggestions for Further Reading

1. GENERAL OVERVIEWS

Adler, David A. *We Remember the Holocaust*. New York: Holt, 1989.

Altshuler, David A. *Hitler's War Against the Jews — the Holocaust: A Young Reader's Version of the War Against the Jews, 1933–1945 by Lucy Dawidowicz*. West Orange, N.J.: Behrman House, 1978.

Chaikin, Miriam. *A Nightmare in History: The Holocaust 1933–1945*. Boston: Houghton Mifflin, 1987.

Meltzer, Milton. *Never to Forget: The Jews of the Holocaust*. New York: Dell Publishing Company, 1977.

Rogasky, Barbara. *Smoke and Ashes: The Story of the Holocaust*. New York: Holiday House, 1988.

Rossell, Seymour. *The Holocaust: The Fire That Raged*. New York: Franklin Watts, 1990.

2. SPECIALIZED TOPICS — NONFICTION

Abells, Chana. *Children We Remember*. New York: Greenwillow, 1986.

Bernstein, Victor. *The Holocaust: Final Judgment*. New York: Macmillan, 1980.

Friedman, Ina. *The Other Victims: First-Person Stories of Non-Jews Persecuted by the Nazis*. Boston: Houghton Mifflin, 1990.

Landau, Elaine. *Warsaw Ghetto Uprising*. New York: Macmillan, 1992.

Meltzer, Milton. *Rescue: The Story of How Gentiles Saved Jews in the Holocaust*. New York: HarperCollins Children's Books, 1991.

Stadtler, Bea. *The Holocaust: A History of Courage and Resistance*. West Orange, N.J.: Behrman House, 1975.

3. BIOGRAPHIES

Atkinson, Linda. *In Kindling Flame: The Story of Hannah Senesh, 1921–1944*. New York: William Morrow, 1992.

Bernheim, Mark. *Father of the Orphans: The Story of Janusz Korczak*. New York: Dutton Children's Books, 1989.

Marrin, Albert. *Hitler: A Portrait of a Tyrant*. New York: Viking, 1987.

Nicholson, Michael, and David Winner. *Raoul Wallenberg*. Ridgefield, Conn.: Morehouse, 1990.

4. FICTION

Gehrts, Barbara. *Don't Say a Word*. New York: Macmillan, 1986.

Laird, Christa. *Shadow of the Wall*. New York: Greenwillow, 1990.

Moskin, Marietta. *I Am Rosemarie*. New York: Dell Publishing Company, 1987.

Orgel, Doris. *The Devil in Vienna*. New York: Puffin, 1988.

Orlev, Uri. *The Man from the Other Side*. Boston: Houghton Mifflin, 1991.

Ramati, Alexander. *And the Violins Stopped Playing: A Story of the Gypsy Holocaust*. New York: Franklin Watts, 1986.

Richter, Hans P. *Friedrich*. New York: Puffin, 1987.

5. MEMOIRS

Auerbacher, Inge. *I Am a Star: Child of the Holocaust*. New York: Prentice Hall, 1987.

Drucker, Olga Levy. *Kindertransport*. New York: Holt, 1992.

Frank, Anne. *The Diary of a Young Girl*. New York: Pocket Books, 1953.

Isaacman, Clara, and Joan A. Grossman. *Clara's Story*. Philadelphia: Jewish Publication Society, 1984.

Koehn, Ilse. *Mischling, Second Degree: My Childhood in Nazi Germany*. New York: Puffin Books, 1990

Reiss, Johanna. *The Upstairs Room*. New York: HarperCollins, 1990.

Roth-Hanno, Renee. *Touch Wood: A Girlhood in Occupied France*. New York: Puffin Books, 1989.

Sender, Ruth M. *The Cage*. New York: Macmillan, 1986.

Wiesel, Elie. *Night*. New York: Bantam, 1982.

Zar, Rose. *In the Mouth of the Wolf*. Philadelphia: Jewish Publication Society, 1983.

6. ART

Bernbaum, Israel. *My Brother's Keeper: The Holocaust Through the Eyes of an Artist*. New York: Putnam, 1985.

Innocenti, Roberto. *Rose Blanche*. New York: Stewart, Tabori and Chang, 1991.

United States Holocaust Memorial Museum. *The Story of Karl Stojka*: A *Childhood in Birkenau*. Washington: D.C.: United States Holocaust Memorial Museum, 1992.

Volavkova, Hana, ed. *I Never Saw Another Butterfly: Children's Drawings and Poems from Terezín Concentration Camp, 1942–1944*. New York: Schocken, 1993.

FOR MORE ADVANCED READERS

1. GENERAL OVERVIEWS

Bauer, Yehuda, and Nili Keren. A *History of the Holocaust*. New York: Franklin Watts, 1982.

Gilbert, Martin. *The Holocaust*: A *History of the Jews in Europe during the Second World War*. New York: Henry Holt, 1986.

Hilberg, Raul. *The Destruction of the European Jews* (student text). New York: Holmes and Meier, 1985.

Yahil, Leni. *The Holocaust: The Fate of European Jewry, 1932–1945*. New York: Oxford, 1991.

2. SPECIALIZED TOPICS — NONFICTION

Adelson, Alan, and Robert Lapides, eds. *Lodz Ghetto: Inside a Community under Siege*. New York: Viking Penguin, 1991.

Allen, William S. *The Nazi Seizure of Power: The Experience of a Single German Town, 1922–1945*. Revised edition. New York: Franklin Watts, 1984.

Arad, Yitzhak. *Ghetto in Flames*. New York: Holocaust Publications, 1982

Block, Gay, and Malka Drucker. *Rescuers: Portraits of Moral Courage in the Holocaust*. New York: Holmes and Meier, 1992.

Conot, Robert E. *Justice at Nuremberg*. New York: Carroll and Graf, 1984.

Des Pres, Terrence. *The Survivor: An Anatomy of Life in the Death Camps*. New York: Oxford University Press, 1976.

Flender, Harold. *Rescue in Denmark*. New York: Anti-Defamation League, 1963.

Friedman, Philip. *Their Brothers' Keepers: The Christian Heroes and Heroines Who Helped the Oppressed Escape the Nazi Terror.* New York: Anti-Defamation League, 1978.

Josephs, Jeremy. *Swastika over Paris: The Fate of the Jews in France.* New York: Arcade Publishing, 1989.

Mayer, Milton. *They Thought They Were Free: The Germans, 1933–1945.* Chicago: University of Chicago Press, 1966.

Patterson, Charles. *Anti-Semitism: The Road to the Holocaust and Beyond.* New York: Walker and Company, 1988.

Plant, Richard. *The Pink Triangle: The Nazi War Against Homosexuals.* New York: Henry Holt, 1986.

Read, Anthony, and David Fisher. *Kristallnacht: The Tragedy of the Nazi Night of Terror.* New York: Random House, 1989.

Rittner, Carol, and Sondra Meyers, eds. *The Courage to Care: Rescuers of Jews During the Holocaust.* New York: New York University Press, 1989.

Szner, Zvi, and Alexander Sened, eds. *With a Camera in the Ghetto.* New York: Schocken, 1987.

3. BIOGRAPHIES

Bierman, John. *Righteous Gentile: The Story of Raoul Wallenberg, Missing Hero of the Holocaust.* New York: Anti-Defamation League, 1981.

Breitman, Richard, and Laqueur, Walter. *Breaking the Silence.* New York: Simon and Schuster, 1986.

Lifton, Betty Jean. *The King of Children: A Portrait of Janusz Korczak.* New York: Schocken, 1989.

Scholl, Inge. *The White Rose: Munich, 1942–43.* Hanover, N.H.: University Press of New England, 1983.

4. FICTION

Appelfeld, Aharon. *To the Land of the Cattails.* New York: Weidenfeld and Nicolson, 1986.

Fink, Ida. *A Scrap of Time.* New York: Schocken, 1989.

Friedlander, Albert. *Out of the Whirlwind.* New York: Schocken, 1989.

Glatstein, Jacob. *Anthology of Holocaust Literature.* New York: Macmillan, 1973.

Lustig, Arnold. *Darkness Casts No Shadows.* Evanston, Ill.: Northwestern University Press, 1985.

Ozick, Cynthia. *The Shawl.* New York: Random House, 1990.

Spiegelman, Art. *Maus* [vols. 1 and 2]. New York: Pantheon, 1991.

Uhlman, Fred. *Reunion.* New York: Farrar, Straus and Giroux, 1977.

5. MEMOIRS

Gies, Miep. *Anne Frank Remembered: The Story of the Woman Who Helped to Hide the Frank Family.* New York: Simon and Schuster, 1988.

Gurdus, Luba K. *The Death Train.* New York: Holocaust Publications, 1987.

Leitner, Isabella. *Fragments of Isabella: A Memoir of Auschwitz.* New York: Dell, 1983.

Levi, Primo. *Survival in Auschwitz.* New York: Macmillan, 1987.

Meed, Vladka. *On Both Sides of the Wall.* New York: Holocaust Publications, 1979.

Nir, Yehuda. *The Lost Childhood.* San Diego: Harcourt Brace Jovanovich, 1991.

Tec, Nechama. *Dry Tears: The Story of a Lost Childhood.* New York: Oxford University Press, 1984.

Yoors, Jan. *Crossing: A Journal of Survival and Resistance in World War II.* New York: Simon and Schuster, 1971.

Tiles created by American
schoolchildren. *Photo*: USHMM.

GLOSSARY

ALLIES: Twenty-six nations led by Britain, the United States, and the Soviet Union that joined in war against Nazi Germany, Italy, Japan, and their allies, known as the Axis powers.

ANTISEMITISM: Prejudices toward Jews or discrimination against them.

ARYAN: Originally, a term for peoples speaking the languages of Europe and India. Twisted by Nazis, who viewed those of Germanic background as the best examples of "superior," "Aryan race."

AUSCHWITZ-BIRKENAU: Largest Nazi camp, located 37 miles west of Cracow, Poland. Established in 1940 as a concentration camp, it included a killing center, at Birkenau, in 1942. Also part of the huge camp complex was I. G. Farben's slave labor camp, known as Buna-Monowitz.

BEŁŻEC: Nazi extermination camp in eastern Poland where an estimated 550,000 Jews were killed between March 1942 and December 1942. Earlier, Bełżec functioned as a forced-labor camp.

BERGEN-BELSEN: Located in northern Germany, transformed from a prisoner-exchange camp into a concentration camp in March 1944. Poor sanitary conditions, epidemics, and starvation led to deaths of thousands, including Anne and Margot Frank in March 1945.

BUCHENWALD: Concentration camp in north-central Germany, established in July 1937. One of the largest concentration camps on German soil, with more than 130 satellite labor camps. It held many political prisoners. More than 65,000 of approximately 250,000 prisoners perished at Buchenwald.

CHANCELLOR: Chief (prime) minister of Germany, head of the government.

CHEŁMNO: Nazi extermination camp in western Poland where at least 150,000 Jews, about 5,000 Gypsies, and several hundred Poles, as well as Soviet prisoners of war, were killed between December 1941 and March 1943 and between April and August 1944.

CONCENTRATION CAMPS: In German, *Konzentrationslager*. Prison camps constructed to hold Jews, Gypsies, political and religious opponents, resisters, homosexuals, and other Germans considered "enemies of the state." Before the end of World War II, more than 100 concentration camps had been created across German-occupied Europe.

DACHAU: First concentration camp, established in March 1933 near Munich, Germany. At first Dachau held only political opponents, but over time, more and more groups were imprisoned there. Thousands died at Dachau from starvation, maltreatment, and disease.

DEATH CAMP: Term widely used to describe both extermination camps, such as Auschwitz-Birkenau and Treblinka, where people were murdered in assembly-line style by gassing, and concentration camps such as Bergen-Belsen and Dachau, without gas chambers but where thousands were killed by starvation, disease, and maltreatment.

DRANCY: Located near Paris, Drancy became the largest transit camp for deportation of Jews from France. Between July 1942 and August 1944, about 61,000 Jews were transported from Drancy to Auschwitz, where most of them perished.

EICHMANN, Adolf (1906–1962): SS Lieutenant Colonel and head of the Gestapo department dealing with Jewish affairs. Organized transports of Jews from all over Europe to Nazi extermination camps. After the war, he escaped to Latin America. Captured by the Israeli Secret Service in Argentina, he was brought to Israel for trial. He was tried in Jerusalem in 1961, convicted, and executed.

EINSATZGRUPPEN: Mobile units of SS and SD (Security Service) which followed German armies into the Soviet Union in June 1941. They were ordered to shoot all Jews, as well as Communist leaders and Gypsies. At least one million Jews were killed by *Einsatzgruppen*.

EXTERMINATION CAMPS: In German, *Vernichtungslager*. Nazi camps, equipped with gassing facilities, for mass murder of Jews. Located in Poland at Auschwitz-Birkenau, Bełżec, Chełmno, Majdanek-Lublin, Sobibór, and Treblinka. Up to 2,700,000 Jews were murdered at these six camps, as were tens of thousands of Gypsies, Soviet prisoners of war, Poles, and others.

FINAL SOLUTION: Refers to "the final solution to the Jewish question in Europe." Nazi code for physical destruction of European Jews.

FRANK, Anne (1929-1945): Born in Frankfurt, Germany. In 1933, she moved with her family to Amsterdam, Holland. On July 6, 1942, they went into hiding and, helped by Miep Gies, remained in hiding until their arrest by Gestapo on August 4,1944. They were held at the Westerbork transit camp from August 8, 1944 until September 3, 1944, when they were deported to Auschwitz-Birkenau. Anne's mother, Edith Frank, perished there on January 6, 1945. Anne and her sister, Margot, were transferred to Bergen-Belsen in late October 1944, and they both died there of typhus in March 1945. Anne's father, Otto Frank, survived.

FÜHRER: German word for "leader."

GENOCIDE: Deliberate, systematic destruction of a racial, cultural, or political group.

GESTAPO: In German, *Geheime Staatspolizei*. Secret State Police.

GOEBBELS, Paul Josef (1897–1945): Minister of propaganda in Nazi Germany, who was close to Hitler. At the end of the war, Goebbels and his wife took their own lives and those of their six children.

GYPSIES: Popular term for Roma and Sinti, nomadic people believed to have come originally from northwest India. Traveling mostly in small caravans, Gypsies first appeared in western Europe in the 1400s and eventually spread to every country of Europe. Prejudices toward Gypsies were and are widespread. Approximately 250,000 to 500,000 Gypsies are believed to have perished in Nazi concentration camps, killing centers, and in E*insatzgruppen* and other shootings.

HEYDRICH, Reinhard (1904-1942): SS Lieutenant General, head of the Reich Security, which included the Gestapo. Organized the E*insatzgruppen* and led the Wannsee Conference of January 1942, where the coordination of the "final solution" was discussed. He was shot by members of the Czech resistance on May 27, 1942, near Prague, and died several days later. To honor Heydrich, Nazis gave the code name "Operation Reinhard" to destruction of the Jews in occupied Poland, at Bełżec, Sobibór, and Treblinka extermination camps.

HIMMLER, Heinrich (1900–1945): Reich leader of the SS from 1929 to 1945, during World War II, he was head of a vast empire: all SS formations, police forces, concentration and labor camps. The senior SS leader responsible for carrying out the "final solution," Himmler committed suicide before he could be brought to trial.

JEHOVAH'S WITNESSES: Religious sect that originated in the United States and had about 20,000 members in Germany in 1933. Witnesses, whose religious beliefs did not allow them to swear allegiance to any worldly power, were persecuted as "enemies of the state." About 10,000 Witnesses from Germany and other countries were imprisoned in concentration camps. Of these, about 2,500 died.

JEWISH COUNCIL: In German, Judenrat. Council of Jewish leaders established on Nazi orders in German-occupied towns and cities.

JUDEN: German word for "Jews."

KILLING CENTERS: Camps equipped with facilities to kill with poisonous gas: Bełżec, Chełmno, Sobibór, Treblinka, as well as killing sections of Auschwitz-Birkenau and Majdanek-Lublin concentration camps.

ŁÓDŹ: Before World War II, a major industrial city in western Poland with a Jewish population second only to Warsaw's. In April 1940, the first major ghetto was created there. Some 43,500 persons died in the Łódź ghetto from starvation, disease, and exposure to cold. Thousands more taken from the ghetto were killed by gassing at Chełmno. In August-September 1944, the 60,000 remaining Jews were sent to Auschwitz.

MAJDANEK-LUBLIN: Located near Lublin in eastern Poland, at first a labor camp for Poles and prisoner-of-war camp for Soviets, it existed as a concentration camp from April 1943 to July 1944. Tens of thousands perished there from starvation, maltreatment, and shootings. Also a killing center, where at least 50,000 Jews were gassed.

MAUTHAUSEN: Concentration camp for men near Linz in upper Austria, opened in August 1938. Many political prisoners were held at Mauthausen and its numerous subcamps. Classified by the SS as one of the two harshest concentration camps; many prisoners were killed there by being pushed from 300-foot cliffs into stone quarries.

MENGELE, Josef (1911–1979): Senior SS physician at Auschwitz-Birkenau from 1943 to 1944. One of the physicians who carried out "selections" of prisoners upon arrival at camp, separating those assigned to forced labor and those to be killed. Mengele also carried out cruel research on twins deported to the camp. After the war, he disappeared. The corpse of a Wolfgang Gerhard, who died in a swimming accident in 1979, was discovered in Brazil in 1985 and identified as Mengele

NAZI: Short term for National Socialist German Workers Party, a right-wing, nationalistic, and antisemitic political party formed in 1919 and headed by Adolf Hitler from 1921 to 1945.

OCCUPATION: Control of a country taken over by a foreign military power.

PALESTINE, British Mandate of: Territory assigned to British control in 1920 by terms of a postwar treaty with defeated Turkey; the British mandate was ended on May 15, 1948, when the territory was divided into the State of Israel and the Kingdom of Jordan.

PARTISAN: Member of a resistance group operating secretly within enemy lines, using hit-and-run guerrilla tactics against occupying forces.

PERSECUTION: Act of causing others to suffer, especially those who differ in background or lifestyle or hold different political or religious beliefs.

POGROM: Russian word for "devastation." Organized violence against Jews, often with understood support of authorities.

RAVENSBRÜCK: Concentration camp for women opened in May 1939, 56 miles north of Berlin. An estimated 120,000 prisoners were inmates there, including many political prisoners, Jews, Gypsies, and Jehovah's Witnesses.

REICH: German word for "empire."

REICHSTAG: Germany's lawmaking body, its parliament.

RHINELAND: Demilitarized zone that Allies established after World War I as a buffer between Germany and western Europe.

ROOSEVELT, Franklin Delano (1882-1945): Thirty-second president of the United States, serving from 1933 to 1945.

SA: In German, *Sturmabteilung*. Storm Troopers. Also called "Brownshirts." Members of a special armed and uniformed branch of the Nazi party.

SCAPEGOAT: Person or group of persons unfairly blamed for wrongs done by others.

SHTETL: Yiddish word for small Jewish town or village.

S0BIBÓR: Nazi extermination camp in eastern Poland where up to 200,000 Jews were killed between May 1942 and November 1943.

SONDERKOMMANDO: German word for "special squad." In the context of extermination camps, it refers to units of Jewish prisoners forced to take away bodies of gassed inmates to be cremated and to remove gold fillings and hair.

SS: In German, *Schutzstaffel*. Protection Squad. Units formed in 1925 as Hitler's personal bodyguard. The SS was later built into a giant organization by Heinrich Himmler. It provided staff for police, camp guards, and military units (*Waffen*-SS) serving with the German army.

STAR OF DAVID: Star with six points, symbol of the Jewish religion.

SUDETENLAND: Mainly German-speaking region that was part of Czechoslovakia between the two world wars. Annexed by Germany in October 1938.

THERESIENSTADT: German name for Czech town of Terezin, located about 40 miles from Prague. Nazis used the Theresienstadt ghetto, established in November 1941, as a "model Jewish settlement" to show Red Cross investigators how well Jews were being treated. In reality, thousands died there from starvation and disease, and thousands more were deported and killed in extermination camps.

TREBLINKA: Nazi extermination camp about 50 miles northeast of Warsaw. Up to 750,000 Jews and at least 2,000 Gypsies were killed at Treblinka between July 1942 and November 1943.

UNDERGROUND: Organized group acting in secrecy to oppose the government or, during war, to resist occupying enemy forces.

WARSAW: The capital of Poland, where about 375,000 Jews lived on the eve of World War II. In October–November 1940, Germans established the Warsaw ghetto, into which some 500,000 Jews were crowded. Of these, an average of 5,000 to 6,000 died each month from starvation, disease, exposure to cold, and shootings. Tens of thousands were deported to Treblinka in 1942. After an uprising organized by resistance fighters ended on May 16, 1943, the surviving Jews were deported to Nazi camps.

WEIMAR REPUBLIC: German republic (1919–1933), a parliamentary democracy, established after World War I, with its capital in the city of Weimar.

WESTERBORK: Transit camp in northeastern Holland for almost 100,000 Jews who were deported between 1942 and 1944 to Auschwitz-Birkenau, Sobibór, Theresienstadt, and Bergen-Belsen. Anne Frank and her family were held at Westerbork between August 8, 1944 and September 3, 1944, when they were put on the last transport to Auschwitz.

YIDDISH: A language that combines elements of German and Hebrew, usually written in Hebrew characters and spoken by Jews chiefly in eastern Europe and areas to which eastern Europeans have migrated.

Index

France, 28, 48, 65, 80
  German occupation of, 36
  Jewish population in, 2
  partisan units in, 74
Frank, Anne, 14, 86, 87
Frank, Margot, 14, 86
Frank, Otto, 86
Frankl, Viktor, 79
Freud, Sigmund, 16
Freund, Irene: pictured, xv, 24, 64, 84
Führer, 9, 30

Gani, Joseph: pictured, xiv, 4, 49, 72
gas chambers, 32, 52–53, 54, 56, 72, 73. See also killing centers
genocide, 46–59, 64, 68
German Foreign Ministry, 46, 48
Germany, 28, 30, 36
  after war, 84
  early 1930s, 8
  Gypsies in, 12, 20–21, 48, 60, 84
  under Hitler, 8–10, 14
  homosexuals in, 20, 84
  invades Poland, 30–31, 38
  invades Soviet Union, 38, 42
  Jehovah's Witnesses in, 20
  Jewish population in, 2, 14
  murder of handicapped in, 32
  pogroms in, 24-25
  racism in, 12, 18
  resistance in, 68
  Wannsee Conference in, 46-47
Gestapo (Geheime Staatspolizei), 10, 30, 47, 74
ghettos, 38–39, 64-65, 74
  deportations from, 48–49
  life in, 40
  resistance in, 70–71
Goebbels, Joseph, 16, 24
Great Britain, 27, 80, 82. See also England
Great Depression
  in Germany, 8

  in United States, 26
Greece, 48
Gurs, 64
Gypsies: children, xii
  in concentration camps, 58, 60, 61
  deportation of, 48, 64
  in ghettos, 38
  mass murder of, 32, 42
  persecution of, 20, 21, 84
  sterilization of, 12, 60

Halle, 21
handicapped: murder of, 32-33
  sterilization of, 32-33
Hartheim, 33
Hemingway, Ernest, 16
Heumann, Lore: pictured, xv, 25, 41, 50
Heumann, Margot: pictured, xv, 85
Heydrich, Reinhard, 46
Himmler, Heinrich, 10, 46
Hitler, Adolf, 7, 12, 16, 18, 30, 32
  anniversary celebrations for, 16
  plots to assassinate, 68
  suicide of, 80
  taking power, 8, 10
Hitler Youth, 16
Holland, 2, 28, 36, 48, 86
Hollerith, Herman, 22
Hollerith machine, 22-23
holocaust: defined, xii. See also Holocaust, the
Holocaust, the, xii, xiii, 28, 42, 64
  antisemitism and, 6, 16
  and extermination camps, 46, 48, 52–54, 70, 72, 78–79
  European Jewish population before, 2
  and liberation, 78–79
  mass shootings during, 42–43, 70
  and Nuremberg trials, 80-81
  rescuing Jews from, 64-65
  survivors of, 82-85

homosexuals, 20, 58, 61, 74, 84
Hungary, 2, 36
  deportations from, 48, 49, 50, 51, 66

identity cards: in Nazi Germany, 18
  photoguide for, xiv
  of United States Holocaust Memorial Museum, xiii
I. G. Farben, 56
immigration quotas, 26
informers, 68, 74
International Business Machines (IBM), 22
Israel, 6, 82. See also Palestine
Italy, 2, 36, 48, 74

Jehovah's Witnesses, 20, 58, 60
Jesus Christ, 6
Jewish Council, 40
Jewish Fighting Organization (Z.O.B.; Zydowska Organizacja Bojawa), 70. See also Warsaw ghetto
Jewish Registry, 22
Jews: as athletes, 18
  boycotts against, 14
  in camps, 46-61, 79
  deportations of, 48–51, 64, 70, 72
  discrimination against, 6, 7, 12, 14–18, 20, 24, 27
  in Europe, 2, 6
  genocide of, 46–54, 64, 68
  in Germany, 2, 4, 14, 18, 22, 24, 26, 48
  in ghettos, 38–41, 48, 70
  mass shootings of, 42–43
  Nobel Prizes of, 14
  occupations of, 4, 6
  partisans, 74–75
  and pogroms, 24, 26
Judaism, 6, 18

7

לזכרון תהנה לאחי היקר ר יעקב ני ולבב . מאתי שמואל דוד ישכב וגב
היסט ערדז טן תמוז .

8

9

12

10

11

Star of David

Stars, triangles, and other markings were used by the Nazis to identify their victims. Almost everywhere under Nazi rule, Jews were forced to purchase and wear a six-pointed Star of David whenever they appeared in public. All concentration camp prisoners wore triangular badges that identified them by the nature of their "crime"; many badges also identified the inmate's race or nationality. *Photo*: USHMM.

Wall of Remembrance

Wall of Remembrance. United States Holocaust Memorial Museum.
More than 3,000 handpainted tiles are mounted on this wall as a
memorial to children who were murdered in the Holocaust. The tiles
were created by students from across the United States as an
expression of their feelings about the Holocaust. *Photo by Alan Gilbert
for* USHMM.

Freight car

One of the several types of freight cars used to deport Jews. As many as eighty to one hundred people were crammed into one car. The trains carrying human freight continued to roll even after Allied bombing raids destroyed railroad lines. Trains were re-routed and additional cars were added to fit more people into fewer trains. The deportations sometimes even took priority over the shipment of troops and supplies to battle zones. *Donated by the Polish State Railways. Photo: USHMM.*

Boat

The clandestine rescue of Danish Jews was undertaken at great personal risk. This boat and several others like it were used by one of the earliest rescue operations, organized by a group of Danes code-named the "Helsingor Sewing Club." The escape route they provided, named the "Kiaer Line" after Erling Kiaer, founder of the "Helsingor Sewing Club," enabled several hundred Jews and non-Jewish family members to escape across a narrow strait to the Swedish coast. On each trip, the boat carried 12 to 14 refugees. Kiaer himself was betrayed and arrested in May 1944. *Photo: USHMM.*

Shoes

The "final solution" was not only carefully planned mass murder, but planned theft on a massive scale. Before victims were gassed at the killing centers, the Nazis took all their belongings from them. First to go were money and other valuables; clothes were next. This mass plunder yielded mountains of clothing. Auschwitz-Birkenau and Majdanek together generated nearly 300,000 pairs of shoes, which were distributed among German settlers in Poland and among the inmates of other concentration camps. These shoes were stolen from prisoners in Majdanek. *On loan from the State Museum of Jamdanek, Lublin, Poland. Photo: USHMM.*

Milk can

Oneg Shabbos milk can. In May 1940, historian Emmanuel Ringelblum (1900–1944) began collecting and recording information about the Warsaw ghetto, where he was imprisoned with his family. Later that year, the growing body of records became part of an underground operation code-named *Oneg Shabbos* (Joy of the Sabbath). Hoping to preserve the history of the daily life and destruction of the ghetto, the group collected many items, including underground newspapers, public notices by the Jewish Council, and reports of deportations and resistance activities. They then placed these materials in metal containers, which they hid in various places in the ghetto. Of the three milk cans that were hidden, two were found after the war. This is the second *Oneg Shabbos* milk can, discovered buried in the rubble of a building at 68 Nowolipki Street in Warsaw on December 1, 1950. *On loan from the Jewish Historical Institute, Warsaw, Poland. Photo: USHMM.*

Suitcases

Suitcases confiscated by the Nazis from prisoners who arrived at Auschwitz-Birkenau. Before deportation, owners of these suitcases had been told to print their names on the outsides. Such instructions as well as detailed orders about the kind of clothing to pack (women were to include two summer and two winter dresses, for example), tricked many victims into believing they would survive and by reducing fears, helped the SS control the large numbers of deportees. In fact, most of the deportees were murdered in the gas chambers within hours after their arrival at Auschwitz-Birkenau and the other extermination camps. *On loan from the State Museum of Auschwitz-Birkenau. Photo: USHMM.*

Butterfly toy

Wooden butterfly toy on wheels made by an unknown prisoner in the carpentry workshop at the Theresienstadt ghetto in Czechoslovakia. The toy was based on a drawing by another prisoner, Professor Milos Bic, a Protestant clergyman. In Theresienstadt, the butterfly often symbolized lost freedom; it was a common image in children's own drawings and poetry created in classes taught by artists and writers imprisoned in the ghetto. The toy had to be smuggled out of the workshop into the special barracks where children were housed. This and other clandestine cultural activities were forms of spiritual resistance. *On loan from the Terezín Memorial, Czechoslovakia. Photo:* USHMM.

Pencil sketch

Fantasy. Pencil sketch on tinted paper. The lower right-hand corner is signed "Raja 25." Raja Englanderova was born in Prague on August 25, 1929, and deported to Theresienstadt on January 30, 1942. She lived in house number 25. Most of the 15,000 children deported to Theresienstadt were later murdered at Auschwitz or perished in other camps; Raja was one of the few hundred children who survived. *On loan from the State Jewish Museum in Prague. Photo*: USHMM.

Child's collage

Untitled collage of pasted paper cut-outs by a child imprisoned in the Theresienstadt ghetto. The child's name is unknown. The background of the flower garden probably portrays the old fortress and hilly landscape that lay just beyond the walled ghetto town. *On loan from the State Jewish Museum in Prague. Photo*: USHMM.